# AN LDS GUIDE TO
# MESOAMERICA

Daniel Johnson        Jared Cooper        Derek Gasser

Cedar Fort, Inc.
Springville, Utah

ISBN 13: 978-1-59955-120-3

Published by CFI, an imprint of Cedar Fort, Inc., 2373 W. 700 S., Springville, UT, 84663
Distributed by Cedar Fort, Inc. www.cedarfort.com

LIBRARY OF CONGRESS CATALOGING-IN-PUBLICATION DATA

Johnson, Daniel, 1970-
  An LDS guide to Mesoamerica / Daniel Johnson, Jared Cooper, Derek Gasser.
    p. cm.
  ISBN 978-1-59955-120-3
  1. Book of Mormon—Geography. 2. Yucatán Peninsula—Description and travel. 3. Guatemala—Description and travel. 4. Honduras—Description and travel. 5. Johnson, Daniel, 1970—Travel. 6. Cooper, Jared—Travel. 7. Gasser, Derek—Travel.  I. Cooper, Jared. II. Gasser, Derek. III. Title.
  BX8627.J56 2008
  289.3'22—dc22
                    2008008652


Cover design by Jeremy Beal
Cover design © 2008 by Lyle Mortimer

Printed in the United States of America

10  9  8  7  6  5  4  3  2  1

Printed on acid-free paper

The authors would like to thank their families for their support during this project, as well as those who gave us encouragement and assistance.

# TABLE OF CONTENTS

# WHY GO TO MESOAMERICA?

Since its publication in 1830, many have wondered where the events mentioned in the Book of Mormon took place. Did these cities cover all of the Americas, from North to South? Was the final resting place of the Nephite record also the scene of their final battle, as well as the Jaredites? Or were the locations restricted to a much smaller area? Where is the best place to begin looking for evidences of these long vanished cultures? During the early years of the Church, not much effort was expended in this search, nor was there much understanding of the history of ancient America. A few cryptic and second-hand statements from Joseph Smith notwithstanding, it appears that there was no definite idea among Church leaders or members as to exactly how Book of Mormon locations related to the geography of the Western Hemisphere.

It has been a common belief among Church members that the final events took place in North America. This belief seems to have been greatly influenced by Orson Pratt's teachings[1] and has persisted even to this day. Even before the publication of the Book of Mormon, many outside of Joseph's associates had speculated about an ancient Israelite origin for Native Americans. This was a popular theory at the time for the Moundbuilders, whose remnants were already known to people in the United States. But nothing resembling the great civilizations and advanced cultures mentioned in this unusual book of scripture was known or even suspected by scholars. Everything had to be taken on faith. If Joseph or his associates had invented the stories in the Book of Mormon, they were taking a huge risk, since practically every detail contradicted what was then believed about the history of ancient America. A good example of the then current scholarly opinion can be found in *The History of the Americas* by Dr. William Robertson. In this volume he writes that "America was not peopled by any nation of the ancient continent which had made considerable progress in civilization. . . . The inhabitants of the New World were in a state of society so extremely rude as to be unacquainted with those arts which are the first essays of human ingenuity in its advance toward improvement." He then went so far as to say, "There is not, in all the extent of that vast empire, a single monument or vestige of any building more ancient than the conquest."[2]

So for the moment, let us forget about horses, swords, vineyards, and Old World writing. These alleged anachronisms are far outweighed by the fact that no one in the early 1800s seriously believed that there was any high civilization in the Americas before the arrival of the Spanish. Yet Joseph's audacious little book spoke of ships; great cities with towers, temples, walls, and gates; a multi-leveled society including kings, governors, judges, priests, merchants, lawyers, and military leaders; extensive roads; a high level of handicraft and artistry; sacred writing; great monuments; defensive fortifications; and huge battles in which thousands were killed. Since there was no evidence for any ancient culture of this level known in the Americas, it was easy to imagine Book of Mormon events happening anywhere, or nowhere at all. Today we may know somewhat about the Maya, Aztecs, and Incas, or places such as Chichén Itzá or Tikal, but back when the Book of Mormon first appeared, almost no one in the United States had heard of such people and places.

All of this changed in 1841 with the publication of *Incidents of Travel in Central America, Chiapas, and Yucatan* by John Lloyd Stephens. Stephens was a well-known author and traveler, having previously published accounts of his journeys in the Middle East, Mediterranean, and Europe. In 1839, he and a renowned artist and draughtsman, Frederick Catherwood, went to Mesoamerica to scout out locations for a possible canal linking the Pacific and Atlantic oceans, as well as to investigate stories about the remnants of ancient art lost in the jungles. Although they were not the first to find and document some of these ancient cities, their record was the first to be made widely available to the general public in this country. Earlier accounts of these pre-Columbian ruins were few and far between, existing only in expensive and rare tomes found in Europe. The report by an expedition in 1787 to explore Palenque, led by Captain Antonio del Río, remained locked in Guatemalan archives until it was finally translated and published in London in 1822. This was the first European notice of these kinds of ruins in America, but little attention was paid to it. The king of Spain ordered an expedition to these sites, which was led by Captain Dupaix. His manuscripts were first published decades later in Paris in 1834. However, Stephens wrote that at the time of their first journey, there was no material available concerning most of the sites they visited. His goal was to reproduce his writings and Catherwood's drawings in such an inexpensive form as to place them within reach of the great mass of the reading community, something which until then had not been done.[3] In 1843 *Incidents of Travel in Yucatan*, an account of their second journey to the Mexican peninsula, was published, and with it the floodgates of knowledge were finally opened. The news was out and a new era of American exploration and research was about to begin.

These books were quite popular, sparking much public interest in the subject. This of course came to the attention of Joseph Smith and other Church leaders in Nauvoo, who were no less interested. Excerpts from Stephens's work were reprinted in the *Times and Seasons* while Joseph was acting editor. A well-known statement from these articles reads, "It would not be a bad plan to compare Mr. Stephens's ruined cities with those in the Book of Mormon."[4] Unfortunately, the martyrdom of Joseph and Hyrum a few years later and the forced expulsion of the Saints westward to find a safe haven overshadowed such trivial pursuits. For many decades, the main concern of Church members was survival, first against the harsh elements of their newfound home, then against laws enacted by the government of their very own country.

In order for Church members to seriously compare lands mentioned in the Book of Mormon with geographical sites in the Americas, two things had to happen. First, the scholarly community had to excavate, study, and come to some conclusions about these ancient sites. This was only beginning to happen by the end of the 19th century. Second, LDS scholars had to gain enough educational background in fields such as anthropology, archaeology, and ancient languages to be able to intelligently review and discuss the finds made by other scientists. One step better would be to actively participate in the work itself. This all began to happen in the 20th century. Brigham Young University's anthropology department began to get involved in fieldwork, excavating sites in Mesoamerica. While not uncovering definitive proof of the Book of Mormon's validity, their work is highly esteemed by the archaeological community and has provided the basis for further work and books on the subject.[5] Eventually, LDS scholars and authors such as B. H. Roberts, Hugh Nibley, Paul R. Cheesman, Milton R. Hunter, John L. Sorenson, and others wrote books comparing and contrasting the latest finds from ancient American research with accounts from the Book of Mormon. As new information came forth from archaeological work in the Americas, some long-held traditions and theories about the Book of Mormon had to be seriously re-evaluated and eventually discarded or updated.

As a result of decades of work and study, practically all LDS scholars agree that once Lehi's group reached the promised land, the events in the Book of Mormon took place in Mesoamerica.[6] While there is disagreement on the details, this theory is almost universally accepted. So how did they reach that conclusion? In order to objectively answer the question of where Book of Mormon events took place, the first thing to do is throw out all preconceived notions and stick to just what is written in this record. This will tell us what to look for and when to look for it. The main story begins with Nephi around 600 BC and ends with Moroni around AD 400. The Jaredite section, which is a bit harder to date, goes back about two thousand years earlier. Since the entire Western Hemisphere has been inhabited since prehistoric times, evidences of ancient people can be found almost everywhere. But unless they fit into this timeline, they must be rejected as not directly relating to the Book of Mormon.

Next, it would be helpful to narrow down our search area a bit. Based on a careful reading of how the Book of Mormon describes distances and durations of travel, most LDS scholars are convinced that it refers to an area only a few hundred miles in length and even less in width.[7] For example, there is simply no way that Limhi's group could have mistakenly traveled from Central America up to New York to find the ruins of the Jaredites and back again in the time period mentioned by the text. Again, if the Lamanites took possession of the land southward, the final Nephite battle could not have been thousands of miles away around the hill where the plates were eventually buried. Years would have been spent in just going from place to place.

Now that we have a timeline and a defined search area, what are we looking for? Just based on a general reading of the text, we need to find large, permanent cities; written language; different people with distinct languages and cultures living near each other; formal governments; a high degree of industry and commerce; evidence of large scale warfare; and a temperate climate with geographical features including hills, volcanoes, major rivers, coastlines, wilderness, and large bodies of water. All of these requirements are met by Mesoamerica, which primarily consists of Mexico, Guatemala, Belize, and Honduras.

Therefore, any serious student of the Book of Mormon wanting to visit areas where Nephi, Alma, Samuel the Lamanite, Captain Moroni, and Mormon lived should be prepared to visit the aforementioned countries. The primary cultures that are known from these areas include the Aztecs, Toltecs, Olmecs, and Maya. The Aztecs can immediately be dismissed, since they are a relatively late culture, still at the peak of their power when the Spanish conquerors arrived. The Maya (of which there are many subgroups, each with its own language and history) are one of the ancient groups that still exist today as a distinct culture. Their origins do date back to Book of Mormon times and beyond. All of the sites we visited were ancient Mayan cities. There are literally hundreds of sites scattered all throughout Mesoamerica, some discovered by the Spanish during their invasion of the New World, others found in the past couple of years using such modern technology as satellite imaging. Archaeologists all admit that there must be countless sites still buried by deep jungle yet to be rediscovered.[8] Major sites are easy to reach and have been restored and set up to accommodate many tourists, with nearby amenities such as shops, hotels, public transportation, and restaurants. Others remain less developed, visited only by archaeologists and diehard students of Mayan culture, and only accessible with the help of local guides on lengthy (and expensive) private tours. In many cases, especially in Guatemala, these locations are in extremely remote areas of jungle where roads have not yet been made, so the only ways to get there are by river (where available), horseback, hiking on foot, or a combination of these. In some cases, small airstrips are nearby, so you may be able to charter a private plane.

Which sites should you visit? That all depends on what you want to see, how much time you have, and what kind of vacation you like. We recommend the sites we have been to, obviously. They are a good blend of the major places that everyone sees, some little-known locations that offer an interesting alternative, and sites with peculiar features that will be of particular interest to students of the Book of Mormon. As you compare the various ancient Mayan cities, you will find that the ones most visited by tourists have great pyramids, ornate temples, sprawling palaces, intricate stonework, and massive monuments. Almost without exception, these features are the result of cultures that reached their peak long after the Book of Mormon's story had ended. These are considered as belonging to the Classic era of Mayan history, which lasts from about AD 250 to 900. They are definitely worth seeing, but you should realize there are limits to how many parallels you can draw between them and Book of Mormon sites. Most Book of Mormon history takes place during the Preclassic period, from 1500 BC to AD 250. The Postclassic period began at the end of the Classic and lasted until the arrival of the Spanish, about AD 1520.

Most of the sites in the Yucatán Peninsula (which actually comprises the Mexican states of Yucatán, Quintana Roo, and Campeche) fall into the Classic period. Many of the latest Mayan sites can be found here. A well-known example on the Caribbean coast, Tulum, is considered a Postclassic site and was apparently still inhabited when the Spanish arrived. Many major sites on the peninsula reached their peak in the tenth century, although Chichén Itzá and Uxmal continued prospering at this time and beyond.[9] As you head south toward Guatemala, you will see that the civilizations reached their peak earlier in history. Populations in cities such as Calakmul and Tikal, two bitter rivals, peaked in the eighth century.[10] As you head farther south into the Guatemalan Highlands, you find sites such as Kaminaljuyú that were at their height of progress and influence centuries earlier, into the Preclassic era,[11] well within most of the Book of Mormon's principal timeline. Some of these sites tend to be simpler architecturally than Classic-era sites, when the Maya were at the height of their power. It seems that most of the excavation and restoration work to prepare sites for tourism has been done at the grander, more impressive Classic cities. In the Mayan area, these sites tend to have more monumental pyramids, temples, and palaces that would have required many years to build. The Classic Maya were also driven by the need to document important events on huge stone monuments called stelae. Since these items are a greater draw for tourists, this is where the limited efforts have been concentrated. It is likely that many sites that actually were Book of Mormon locations would not be much to look at today or have been covered up by later construction, even modern cities.

Although all these areas had inhabitants as far back as prehistoric times, there is not much record left from these time periods, at least not what would attract many tourists. The preceding brief description should give you a general idea of where more complex civilizations evolved and spread. Many of the earlier permanent settlements started out near the Pacific coast of Guatemala and southern Mexico. Over the centuries they spread out in all directions. This is an admittedly simplified view, but it does correspond somewhat to the view currently held by most LDS scholars: that Lehi's group landed on the Pacific coast of southern Mexico or southwestern Guatemala. This would then be the origin point of the Nephite and Lamanite cultures.

Of course, there were already people living in these lands at that time. Both the Book of Mormon and accepted archaeology affirm that. While Nephi did not specifically mention any other people, the narrow and specific scope of his record and the fact that it is not complete (remember the 116 pages lost by Martin Harris?) are sufficient to explain this lack of detail. We do know that generations later, the Nephites stumble onto the vestiges and even one survivor of an ancient and hitherto unknown culture, that of the Jaredites. Traditional archaeology also informs us of an ancient people whose roots date back to at least 1200 BC, the Olmecs. Their civilization was primarily centered around central Mexico and its Gulf Coast. Some LDS scholars have suggested a link between the Olmecs and the Jaredites, theorizing that they could have been one and the same.[12] It should be obvious that non-LDS historians would not accept this view, but there are many questions still to be answered about the Olmecs. They appear to be a fully developed culture and have often been referred to as the mother culture of ancient Mesoamerica. However, a more current view is that sites, artifacts, monuments, and writing that had previously all been lumped together under the Olmec classification may actually refer to several different and unrelated peoples.[13] The final conclusion has yet to be reached, but it seems possible that the

Jaredites could fit in there somewhere.

It may be noticed that our book does not deal with any Olmec sites. This is due to the regions we visited during our expedition. It is also because more is known about the Maya and their cities, and for the most part, these areas are quite easy to travel in and are well set up for tourism. It is not difficult to find lots of information about sites like Tikal, Palenque, and Copán. Much of the Mayan hieroglyphs can be read,[14] and many books can be found in most bookstores for studying up on Mayan culture. While not all questions are answered and new findings at times make current beliefs obsolete, there is a good base from which to start. With the Olmecs, it is not so easy. Less is known or published about them, and their writing systems are not fully deciphered. We do hope to turn our attention to this worthy culture someday, and if all goes well, a trip to central Mexico may be forthcoming. Until that time, we will concentrate our efforts on the great Mayan people.

If a possible correlation exists between the Olmecs and the Jaredites, then what about the Maya? They or their ancestors were most likely already in the Americas when Lehi's group arrived, so how do they fit in? A popular idea now is that there may be some connection between the Maya and the Lamanites. It is interesting to note that the Mayan Classic era began as the Book of Mormon account ends. As the Nephite culture was decimated or assimilated by the Lamanites, the Mayan civilization was on the rise. Major cities that can still be seen throughout Mesoamerica were built mainly during this period. Perhaps an influx of cultural ideas and technological advancements from the waning Nephite culture gave the Mayan/Lamanite groups the boost they needed to take their society to the next level. As the dwindling Nephites were being pushed farther northward, the Lamanite culture could have been expanding in the land southward, building up to the great achievements and expansion of their Classic period.

Another possible connection between the Lamanites and the Maya could date back to much earlier in the Book of Mormon history. We know that Nephi was warned to take those who were obedient to the commandments of God and separate themselves from the followers of Laman and Lemuel. Thus began the division of Lehi's group into Nephites and Lamanites, although the definition of these terms changed from time to time throughout the record. Even during Nephi's lifetime, he and his followers were obliged to fight their brethren in order to defend themselves from annihilation. We soon learn that the Lamanites had become quite a different culture in a very short time. They kept no records, they led a technologically more primitive lifestyle, their skin color became darker, and they were cursed by being removed from the covenants of God (by their own disobedience). Most important, they usually appeared to outnumber the Nephites.

How did they become so different and so numerous in a relatively short time? Various theories have been advanced as explanations, but a simple one is that the Lamanites mixed with local cultures already there. When we read that their skin color was changed as a sign for the Nephites, we may be tempted to imagine that they just woke up one morning, looked at each other, and got the shock of their lives. A more likely scenario is that they came upon the Maya or their ancestors and intermarried with them. In a few generations, the descendants of the Lamanites could have been visually indistinguishable from the Maya. It would also have been natural to adapt the culture and habits of those already living in these lands. If they brought some of their own beliefs to the Maya, that could provide the justification for the wars against the Nephites.

Since the Maya still exist as a people today, can any trace of Lamanite traditions be found in their culture? It can, if you know where to look. Many of the Spanish conquerors documented what they found in the New World. Generally, most of these accounts were at first ignored by the rest of the world, but they have been generating more attention and interest in recent decades. There were several Spanish explorers and Catholic priests who wrote of what they encountered on their journeys, but perhaps the best known is Friar Diego de Landa. He was head of the Franciscan order in the newly conquered Yucatán Peninsula. After discovering that many of the native converts to Catholicism were secretly continuing to practice their ancient rituals, he responded by declaring his infamous *Auto de fe* in 1562.[15] Thus he began his own inquisition, torturing and imprisoning those Maya he found guilty, as well as destroying thousands of idols and gathering up all the indigenous writings he could find. Of these, he wrote, "We found a great number of books in these letters, and since they contained nothing but superstitions and falsehoods of the devil we burned them all, which they took most grievously, and which gave them great pain."[16] His persecutions became so severe that complaints eventually reached the king of Spain, and Landa was recalled home to answer for these charges. He justified his actions by writing an account of what he had witnessed in the New World in 1566. The modern English translation is known as *Yucatan Before and After the Conquest*. In it he gives an invaluable view of the Mayan culture that the Spanish found upon their arrival. It is highly ironic that the man responsible for almost completely destroying the Mayan written history has become a crucial source of information about them. Because of him, only a handful of Mayan books or codices exist today, but without his account, we would be left even further in the dark about ancient Mayan beliefs and practices. The following are but a few excerpts from *Yucatan* that should be of particular interest to Latter-day Saints:

# On the Origin of the Maya

"Some old men of Yucatán say that they have heard from their ancestors that this country was peopled by a certain race who came from the East, whom God delivered by opening for them twelve roads through the sea."[17]

# On Their Appearance

"They painted their faces and bodies red, disfiguring themselves. . . .Their clothing was a strip of cloth . . . which they wrapped several times about the waist, leaving one end hang in front and one behind. They wore sandals of hemp or deerskin tanned dry, and then no other garments."[18]

# On Baptism

"Baptism is not found anywhere in the Indies save here in Yucatán. . . . Its origin we have been unable to learn, but it is something they have always used and for which they have had such devotion that no one fails to receive it. . . . The time of baptism . . . was given between the ages of three and twelve."[19]

# On Their Weapons of War

"They had offensive and defensive arms. The offensive were bows and arrows....They had hatchets of a certain metal . . . fastened in a handle of wood. They had short lances.... For defense they had shields made of split and woven reeds, and covered in deer hide. They wore protective jackets of cotton, quilted in double thicknesses, which were very strong. Some of the chiefs and captains wore helmets of wood."[20]

# On Their Religious Teachings

"The most learned of the priests opened a book, and observed the predictions for that year, declared the to those present, preached to them a little enjoining the necessary observances."[21]

# On Their Buildings and Construction

"So many, in so many places, and so well built of stone are they, it is a marvel; the buildings themselves, and their number. . . . There is no memory of the builders, who seem to have been the first inhabitants. [T]here are traces of there having been a fine paved road . . . all the ground about them was paved, traces being still visible, so strong was the cement of which they were made."[22]

From these few observations, it is easy to see some similarities between the ancient cultures of Mesoamerica and details found in the Book of Mormon. Since none of this information was known at the time in the United States, Joseph Smith and his associates were extremely lucky if they were just making this up. It is true that some assertions made by the Book of Mormon are still controversial, in that they cannot be fully explained by our current understanding of ancient America. However, many of these items now have plausible or definite support in the latest findings by even non-LDS archaeologists. We will cover these points in detail in the chapters that deal with specific sites.

What about the Nephites, the people who actually gave us the Book of Mormon? Can any evidence be found for their civilization? They probably would have been the most distinct and unusual group in Mesoamerica, yet supporting evidence for them proves to be the most elusive. This should not be surprising, though. At the end of his record, Mormon tells us that his people had degenerated to the level of their enemies the Lamanites, becoming even more violent and bloodthirsty than their enemies. It appears that after the final battle, they were either destroyed or assimilated. We know that most of their cities were taken over by the Lamanites. Mormon and Moroni had to go to extraordinary lengths to safeguard the records they were working on. They knew that if the Lamanites found them, they would be destroyed because they contradicted the Lamanites' own oral traditions. This tendency to destroy previous or competing records was commonplace among many Mesoamerican cultures, including the Olmecs, the Maya, and the Aztecs. When kings replaced each other or conquered a rival city, they usually destroyed and buried the monuments and burned the records of the previous leaders.[23] Any Nephite records would likely have been destroyed by the victorious Lamanites or so well hidden that they have never been found.

We have a tentative theory regarding the Nephites' place in ancient American history. It is interesting that most of this timeline (600 BC to AD 400) is accompanied by an astounding lack of detail in the historical record. Much more is known about the Mayan Classic period, especially the seventh through the ninth centuries. The great majority of their sculpted writing, stelae, and massive construction dates from this period. Also notable during this era is the influence of the Toltecs, a group that came from Central Mexico. Many references to them describe them as warlike, highly advanced, and bearded. We tentatively suggest that they could be what Nephites became after their complete fall from grace. Those wishing to see remnants of this culture should visit Chichén Itzá.

Although mainstream archaeology does not recognize the possibility of a distinctive Israelite culture in ancient America, so many different peoples lived in these lands and many are still not understood. It is well known that most Classic Mayan cities were built over much earlier, simpler sites that have since been completely obscured. For example, evidence has been found for habitation at the site of Tikal in Guatemala that dates back to at least 600 BC. These were much simpler, perishable structures, but who built them, where they came from, or what they called themselves or their settlement is still unknown.[24] So much has happened in this relatively small area that has been lost forever, as will be shown later in this book. In addition, so much of Mesoamerica remains in its wild state, and American archaeology is still in its infancy when compared to the rest of the word. With this in mind, it is best to refrain from final judgment on the currently unanswerable questions about the Book of Mormon. The most important question will only be answered through faith.

This brings us to an important question: Did we find proof that the Book of Mormon is true?

Our answer to that would have to be yes and no. It seems that people who look to archaeology for a definitive, positive answer end up disappointed. As far as we know, no one has unquestionably found the city of Zarahemla, golden plates written by Nephi, or Captain Moroni's standard of liberty, although some outrageous claims have been made. Just as unlikely are opponents' claims that archaeology has proven the Book of Mormon a modern fraud. This is becoming an increasingly untenable position, given the rate at which previously held beliefs become outdated by new finds. Much of the material gained from ongoing excavations never reaches the general public. And we have not even touched on the philosophical challenges of proving a negative.

What we can say from our limited studies on the subject and travels through these lands is that the events in the Book of Mormon easily could have happened and Mesoamerica is the most likely candidate for its setting. There still exist holes in our understanding of how some things relate to ancient America. Honestly, we will probably never have a good answer for every challenge the critics may throw our way. But there are surprisingly strong answers to many of them, and as excavations in Mesoamerica progress, more supporting evidence gathers. Most objections to the Book of Mormon nowadays come from a position of ignorance. If we grow frustrated at the lack of knowledge shown by our detractors, we certainly should not excuse it in ourselves. We have found some amazing things on our journeys and are surprised that more people are not talking about them. We would like all these things to become common knowledge. Not only does that support our position, but it honors the great and noble cultures of the American past that have for so long been ignored or underestimated. We wish to shout these things from the rooftops so that a dialog may begin between scholars and laypersons alike. Too much time is wasted debating issues like horses, cement, swords, and transoceanic voyages, which are already moot points. There are so many more vital and interesting points to consider. If we can find such unexpected evidences for the Book of Mormon, what else lies hidden in the jungles, just waiting to be rediscovered? As Diego de Landa himself said, "It may be that this country holds a secret that up to the present has not been revealed, or which the natives of today cannot tell."[25]

# THE BOOK'S PURPOSE

Over the past several years we have amassed quite a library of books about ancient America and the Maya. Our collection ranges from the historical and archaeological, written by respected experts in their fields, to books and articles written from an LDS perspective about the connections between Mesoamerica and the peoples mentioned in the Book of Mormon. It was a challenge to find a single source that had an in-depth explanation of each ruin in the area. By far the best source we found was *Archaeological Mexico,* written by Andrew Coe. This was an impressive book, focusing not only on the Maya but also on many major archaeological sites in Mexico, including Olmec, Aztec, and others. We have found nothing near that quality for Guatemala or other Central American countries.

Finding a single source that would provide us detailed information on a site-by-site basis from an LDS perspective was impossible. In fact, often we would read about interesting artifacts in LDS literature that could relate to the Book of Mormon, but found it extremely difficult to determine where these artifacts are now. Many books about ancient America and the Book of Mormon have tantalizing pictures of carvings, paintings, or objects that would appear to have a connection to this book of scripture, but rarely are there explanations of their context or a description of where they might be located.

For example, the Mayan hieroglyph for "it came to pass" was mentioned in some LDS publications, but only one vague location was given for this glyph. In order to ensure that we would see it on our journeys, we had to learn about it on our own, reading about its meanings and different forms from various pieces of archaeological literature. Often, these are very dry and detail-oriented books and reports that are hard for the average person to get through. Once empowered with our new expertise on this one Mayan glyph, we started searching for it by studying as much Mayan glyphic writing as we could find. Our search first led us to Stela 3 found at Piedras Negras in Guatemala, which caused us to consider changing our travel plans so that we could go to this remote site and see the four instances of this glyph that we considered so rare at the time. We contacted Stephen Houston, a respected archaeologist currently at Brown University who had excavated the site, to see where this stela was currently located. To our dismay we learned from him that the stela had been broken apart and stolen by looters, presumably for sale on the black market.[1]

Disappointed, we decided we would stick to our original travel plans and continued our search for the glyph. We knew that it was somewhere at Palenque, but we were not sure we would be able to fit a visit into our itinerary. With relief, we discovered that we would find this glyph at a site called Yaxchilán, near Piedras Negras, but much more accessible. One of the biggest surprises of our trip to Guatemala, Mexico, and Honduras was that the glyph for "it came to pass" could be found almost everywhere we found Mayan writing. While we were pleased that our search had yielded positive results and had also forced us to learn more about Mayan writing and how to read some of it, it was frustrating that we had not read about this fact in any of our books by LDS scholars. Even LDS tour groups commented on how they would try and find the glyph at the top of the Temple of Inscriptions at Palenque, which was actually inaccessible because it is now closed to the public. Yet all you need to do is walk into the museum or look at the Temple of the Cross, or the Foliated Cross, or the Sun; it is literally almost everywhere.

Even more frustrating was the fact that we found many similarities to the Book of Mormon in our studies that were not mentioned in LDS books and articles we were reading as we began to write our book. For instance, we initially learned of gold plates with Mayan designs and hieroglyphic writing that were found in the cenote of Chichén Itzá from a brief mention in *Archaeological Mexico*.[2] When we really looked into it, we found that not just one or two, but over 29 plates or disks have been found. We searched for weeks to find out where we could see them and eventually learned that most of them resided in the Peabody museum at Harvard. We were lucky enough to get an appointment for a research visit to see those artifacts and were shocked to hear that they were not on display, but rather were kept in storage. Gold plates with ancient writing on them found in Mesoamerica? These are not controversial claims of dubious origin, but rather widely accepted finds that have been known for almost a century. We just cannot understand why more people, especially in the Church, are not discussing these finds. However, as we were completing this book, we found that Dr. John L. Lund mentioned these same gold disks in his recent work, *Mesoamerica and the Book of Mormon: Is This the Place?* We were pleased to see another LDS author refer to them and hope that they will someday receive more attention and study.

Perhaps we should make it clear that we are not scholars or historians. We are not experts in Mayan history or archaeology, but we are very interested in these topics and have developed almost an obsession for them. We enjoy traveling to other countries and experiencing cultures foreign to our own. Our wish in writing this book is to provide the traveler to Mesoamerica a single, easy-to-read reference point on the Maya, from an LDS perspective and on a site-by-site basis. To accomplish this goal, we have poured over many different books, reports, and periodicals on Mesoamerican archaeology to find and distill out the salient points that would be of greatest interest to the LDS traveler or student of the Book of Mormon. We worked hard to ensure that our information came from credible sources and respected Mayan scholars and archaeologists such as Michael Coe, Linda Schele, Peter Mathews, Nikolai Grube, Tatiana Proskouriakoff, and others. From these sources, we made our connections between Mesoamerica and the Book of Mormon.

Most of our ideas and connections are not new and are not our own, but rather represent the latest thinking by respected and renowned scholars in the field. Yet some of our conclusions are a result of our own reasoning from our studies and experiences. At the very least, we have not come across them yet in our continuing study of the LDS and non-LDS theories about these cultures. Some of the observations and possibilities we present in this book are to be found nowhere else, but all are based on what we have seen and gleaned from acknowledged experts.

We do not claim these connections as absolute fact and would not be devastated to learn that we were completely wrong (well, maybe just a little). Often, the study of Mesoamerica has followed this same pattern. Much of what is currently believed about ancient America and its peoples directly contradicts the opinions held only a few decades ago. It is a fascinating time to be studying the Maya and other cultures, whether or not there is any connection to the Book of Mormon, as so much is still being discovered and public interest in them seems to be increasing. We do feel that Mesoamerica would be the most likely setting for the Book of Mormon; there are just too many similarities to ignore. In our view, each new discovery has brought the connection between Mesoamerica and the Book of Mormon closer and closer. Regardless of what the future still holds, we hope that this book provides travelers much of the information that they would need to make their trip or even their studying all the more interesting and insightful.

Even for those who may never travel to these lands, we hope this book proves to be beneficial. Our experiences and mishaps, both good and bad, should make for some interesting stories. This is not a scholarly treatise, and we would not presume to compare it with the groundbreaking and dedicated work done by so many competent Mesoamerican scholars, both within the Church and without. We are immensely indebted to the trails they have blazed and the light they have shed on these fascinating ancient cultures. We wish to make their discoveries and theories known and show how closely some of them relate to the Book of Mormon. Too often, their findings are not widely disseminated. And when they are, it is usually in very technical writings full of unrecognizable (and unpronounceable) names, dates consisting of long strings of numbers, and places with such unmemorable names as Structure 2A or Group XIX. This book assembles an overall understanding of these cultures so that the average layperson can appreciate them and see for himself what does and does not relate to the Book of Mormon. As interested students of these cultures, our perspective and experience can help to accomplish that.

You may notice that we do not give very detailed travel information like addresses, phone numbers, prices, bus schedules, and the like. That is not the intent of this book. If you do plan a trip to Mesoamerica, you should definitely invest in a few good travel guides. Better yet, find friends or acquaintances who have gone there and ask them about their experiences. We want to give you information you will not find in the guidebooks because we cannot compete with them. We hope instead to supplement them and tell you the kinds of things you wish they would. We also want to provide details that would be of interest to the LDS traveler and tell you of our real-world experiences there, hoping they may be of some benefit on your own excursion. You can then compare your adventure to ours. Along the way, we intend to make our story an interesting and engaging read, something for which you would not usually pick up a travel guide.

# GETTING THERE: GUATEMALA CITY

## Disclaimer

We are not professional travelers or scholars. Any information we give is accurate to the best of our knowledge, but it is based on our own experiences of travel in January of 2007. Much of the information we read during our planning stages turned out to be obsolete or not applicable by the time we got there. There is also a certain amount of luck involved. Our experiences, both good and bad, may not be your experiences. We did find Guatemala to be rougher and with less infrastructure for tourists than Mexico or Honduras. Use our account as a guide but not the final word. As always, if you are traveling to a foreign country, check out the latest advisories for travelers abroad and get the most current information you can. The warnings for crimes against travelers in Guatemala sounded pretty extreme to us, but we did not experience any problems. Still, you should be cautious and expect the unexpected.

Between the Pacific and Atlantic Oceans lies a narrow piece of land full of mountains, volcanoes, lakes, and lots of Mayan history. Guatemala is a beautiful country both from its physical characteristics and the kind demeanor of its people. After traveling through the country we were both amazed and impressed by the friendly attitudes of those we encountered. Not that those in Mexico were not friendly; it just seemed that the Guatemalans went out of their way to make us feel welcome.

## Arriving in Guatemala City

If you base your first impression of Guatemala on its airport, you may be less than impressed. Guatemala City's Aeropuerto La Aurora is the country's major international airport and one of just two in the country that have international flights. The Flores International Airport is located in the north and could be a convenient arrival point if you were visiting only sites in the Petén. Unfortunately this airport has few flights to and from the United States and is becoming less available. But on a shorter trip with less time to travel across the country, this option could be extremely convenient. The Guatemala City Airport is rather small and looks as if it has been in use for some time with little repair or renovation. It does serve its purpose but may come as a shock to those who have not traveled much outside of the United States.

Our flight arrived at the airport late in the evening. After filling out the necessary forms and going through customs, we ended up at the small baggage claim to wait for our luggage. We had planned on camping several nights and brought tents and sleeping bags, thus requiring us to check our bags. It is much less risky to not check your bags and carry them onboard if at all possible. We waited anxiously for our bags and gear to appear, and as the hour grew later and later, we were contemplating what we would do without our camping gear. Then one bag appeared, followed by another, and finally another. Around midnight, all of our luggage had arrived and we breathed a silent sigh of relief. Perhaps that is just the way things work here. So be prepared to wait a while for your luggage and do not become concerned if it does not show up immediately.

One positive note about the airport is the tourist services counter, located near the baggage claim. A nice young man was manning it and gave us some helpful information, including informing us that ATMs were down citywide due to a shortage of cash. Shortly after learning about our cash crisis we became concerned that the hotel we had booked a room at somehow did not show our reservation. The young man behind the service counter offered to call our hotel for us, but there was no answer. After several attempts and with midnight approaching, we realized we were calling the wrong place and finally found the right number. Relieved to find a hotel where our reservation did indeed exist, we set out on foot, loaded up with all our luggage but without any local cash.

We spent our first night at a hotel that was close to the airport. Although it was theoretically within walking distance, it seemed like a long hot trek carrying all of our gear. Even late at night and with a bit of a breeze, we could definitely feel the humidity. The airport is located in the southern part of the city in Zone 13. Zones 13 and 14 contain many of these hotels and guesthouses that could serve as a starting point for your trip. We stayed at the Aeropuerto Guesthouse, which  is in a residential neighborhood a few blocks from the airport in a house that the owners had converted to receive travelers. The yard was surrounded by a fence and locked gate, not uncommon in urban precincts in this area. We rang the buzzer and were let in. Our intent was to pay with a credit card, which they did accept, but we were informed that the network for the machines had been down most of the day. Perhaps there was some connection with the lack of cash for the ATMs. We asked the owner to try anyway and to our relief it worked; we were able to pay for the room without using cash. Our upstairs room included its own bathroom and was a good, economical place to stay for the night. Breakfast the next morning was included in the bill.

Once again, if you have not traveled much outside of the United States, the rooms may come as a little bit of a shock. Most of our rooms were clean but definitely on a different standard than you would find in more developed countries. Because of the heat and humidity, most rooms come standard with a small fan to keep you cool during the night. One hotel we stayed at in the Petén jungle had a generator that powered the hotel during the day until 10:00 at night. At this time, the power went off and we were on our own with no lights or fan. While the rooms did serve their purpose, they felt more like a mix between camping and spending a night at an old Motel 6. On our last night in the country and perhaps feeling a bit homesick, we splurged and ate dinner at a Pizza Hut and stayed at the Marriott in Guatemala City, which was pleasantly not very expensive. After many nights of cheaper accommodations and camping, it was a nice, comfortable ending to a wonderful trip.

## Using Money

Conveniently located next to the baggage claim was a shiny new ATM. After several attempts to retrieve cash we were surprised with the repeated message: "ATM out of Cash." Thinking this must be a mistake, we spoke to someone at the tourist desk. He told us Guatemala City was currently experiencing a shortage of cash and no one knew when it would be available. Thankfully, we were able to find multiple ATMs the next day, and yes, they did have cash. They seemed to be readily available in most areas of Guatemala. This greater access to cash did not help one of us, who had specifically called his credit card company beforehand to advise them he would be using his card in Guatemala, only to find that it did not work in any Guatemalan ATM. In this case, banks are an acceptable, if less convenient, means of obtaining necessary funds.

Credit cards are nice to have, but unless you restrict your spending to the more touristy areas that cater to foreign travelers, do not count on being able to use them often to make purchases. Traveler's checks are practically useless, so we do not recommend them at all. Oddly enough, even U.S. dollars in cash are really not that helpful in some remote areas. You will need to find a bank or person to exchange them, and as we found out, that can be a challenge at times. So plan on using local currency in most situations. If you do follow our route, you will be passing through remote localities, eating at local restaurants, and shopping at little markets and souvenir stands, all of which will require payment in quetzals, pesos, or lempiras. In paying for curios and some services, bartering is quite expected and just part of the way things work, so give it a try; you can usually get a lower price than the first one offered.

## Traveling Around the Country

Although renting a car is more expensive and introduces some inherent risks, it is a far more convenient way to see multiple sites with much more freedom. Without a car there simply is no way to see the remote sites or visit several in a reasonable amount of time. You are able to drive in Guatemala with your home country's driver's license or an international driving permit. As you are exiting the airport, you will come to an open area with lots of small rental car booths on the left. Hopefully your rental car agency has someone working the booth who can instruct you to fill out the paperwork, and more important, find your car. In our case we returned the next morning to find an empty booth. After waiting for some time, we were greeted by an employee and taken to a shuttle for the car lot. What seemed to be a fairly long drive ended up landing us across the street from the airport. Filling out the necessary paperwork took some time, and we opted to go with full insurance as recommended by several guidebooks. One thing to consider is if you are planning on driving into another country, such as Honduras or Belize, you will need to get a certified documentation from the rental car agency that you have permission to do so. In our case this was an additional charge, but it is the law. We were warned of hefty fines if we were caught driving a rental car in another country without proper documentation.

As we were finishing the paperwork, the agent mentioned that the car we thought we were getting, a new local version of a Mitsubishi Montero Sport, had not been cleaned yet, but not to worry because they had a small pickup truck they would let us take for the same price. This did not seem like a great deal to us. Several days later when it had rained daily for hours at a time, we were thankful we had put up a fight to stick with the SUV. Even though we had not  expected it, we experienced rain most of the days we were there, so the SUV was very helpful, not to mention the peace of mind in having our gear locked (relatively) safely inside.

# If You Drive

Many of the routes we took, combined with the rain, would have been impossible or very dangerous without four-wheel drive capabilities. The Guatemalan jungles are very remote and undeveloped, so roads leading to some sites are merely dirt trails that become muddy or impassible during the rainy season. Arriving during the right time of the year is crucial. Even in remote areas, surprisingly, gas stations were not hard to find, but filling the tank was very expensive. Plan on using cash for gas because most stations do not accept credit cards.

Fortunately for us, our Montero had a diesel engine, unavailable in the United States. The benefits of diesel are well appreciated in many parts of the world, if not in our own country. Generally, it is cheaper than gasoline (petrol) and is a more efficient fuel, yielding more miles per gallon. While refueling the SUV was a major portion of our expenditures, having a diesel vehicle made it less burdensome than it otherwise would have been. We just hope that someday soon more small and midsize vehicles in the Unites States will be available with this option so that we can take advantage of diesel's efficiency like the rest of the world.

17

While most of the driving seemed straight forward, we did run into the same problem in every locale. With no signs posted, finding our way out of cities and towns seemed difficult and confusing. In some cases, we tried multiple routes with directions from the locals and still had problems finding our way out of town. In comparison to Mexico and Honduras, some of the sites in Guatemala took more navigating and were harder to reach. Driving times were usually

different than what we expected, either because of rough roads or getting caught in traffic with slow trucks. In one memorable instance, a road we took was still being built and caused us many delays, even though it appeared complete on our map. Needless to say, we had many surprising and enjoyable times on the roads in Guatemala, as well as a few that were not so enjoyable, but made for entertaining stories once we were safely home.

## Things to Look Out For

In all honesty, we had read some truly frightening accounts of violence against travelers in Guatemala, especially around the volcanoes and in remote areas. Stories of attacks with machetes and carjackings by armed gunmen are enough to dissuade many less hardy travelers. Happily, we can report that we experienced no such trouble and found Guatemalans to be very nice and courteous. Even late at night and in remote jungles, we felt very safe.

More current information indicates that crackdowns by police and military forces have solved many of the problems and removed the dangers to tourists. We passed through one military checkpoint on our travels and found the soldiers to be very courteous. While the country is a bit rougher than in some areas of Mexico, we had a very enjoyable time and would recommend it to almost anyone.

That said, knowing how to travel safely and not stand out as a likely target are very important. Also, being able to speak Spanish proved invaluable in many circumstances. With our rental car, we were able to get to most of our planned destinations on our own, but for crossing the Usumacinta River into Mexico and arranging travel beyond, speaking the language was a necessity. It may have been possible to get there without speaking Spanish, but it would have been much more difficult. In the more remote areas, we did not find anyone who spoke English, so getting a better deal on prices and just knowing what was going on would have been very hard. We took as many precautions as we could and never felt that we were in a dangerous situation. But upon our return, several friends who had been to Guatemala told us that they could not believe that we did not get robbed at least once. So could it be that we were just lucky?

# Food Safety

One more topic on the subject of safety: food. Everyone has heard of Moctezuma's revenge, and those who have had it know it is not very pleasant. Fortunately, it can be easily avoided and you can bring some medications along to alleviate your symptoms. The problem comes from parasites in the water, so if you keep away from tap water, most of the danger is negated. But this means more than not drinking it or using it to brush your teeth. In most cases, you need to avoid ice and uncooked foods that could have been washed in tap water. If you stay in big, touristy places, chances are that hotels and restaurants are already purifying their water, but you should always ask to make sure. Even in smaller local restaurants, you are safe buying a soda or bottled water with your meal. Just be sure to remember this phrase: *sin hielo* (without ice). Food never was a problem for us. We did not buy things off the street, but other than that, we looked for places where the locals ate. You will have a much more authentic experience that way and the food is very tasty.

You may want to know what you can expect to eat in such establishments. Travel books usually have a section on exotic local food found in particular areas. Much of it sounds really interesting, but we do not know where they are finding it, unless they are going to specialty restaurants or finding it during important festivals. What we found was a fairly consistent selection of simple meals. If you have a good grasp of a common Spanish vocabulary for food, you will recognize most of your choices. Most dishes have beef, pork, or chicken, seasoned and cooked or as pieces in some kind of sauce. There will usually be rice or black beans accompanying it. Often a meal comes with French fries, which are actually big wedges of potato fried in oil. They are much better than what you get as a side order to a burger in the U.S. There will sometimes be a little salad, usually pickled carrots, onions, and the like. Everything will come with a plate of little white corn tortillas, just like you might expect bread or rolls with your meal in American restaurants.

The guidelines for eating and drinking safely in Guatemala and Honduras are basically the same as for Mexico. We do not hear as much about ailments for tourists here, but we recommend the same precautions. Keep plenty of bottled water with you and keep hydrated. Luckily, you can get safe water pretty much anywhere. Because of the exertion of wandering all around ruins and climbing tall, steep pyramids in the tropical heat, we recommend a backpack with a built-in water reservoir so you can keep hydrated. This is essential to avoiding heatstroke and exhaustion, and in general will keep you healthier. A neat trick is to bring this type of backpack with you as a carry-on. Before you board your plane leaving the United States, fill it up from a convenient airport water fountain. Then you hit the country with a couple of liters of clean, cool, and free water.

For meals, we mostly ate in small local restaurants. The cuisine in all three countries is similar in many respects, and most of our food was delicious. Many restaurants, especially near large tourist areas, will have some menu items that sound familiar to Americans, but in our experience, these are usually not very good, and you are better off sticking with local fare. An unappetizing meal of spaghetti in a restaurant at Tikal taught us this lesson.

# When You Reach the Sites

We strongly suggest bringing back some nice replicas of ancient artifacts. They look great on your table or bookcase, give your home an air of well-traveled culture, and make great conversation pieces. In all the countries we visited, the sites themselves are usually the best places to find souvenirs. We did not see many tourist shops along the way, so we looked in booths at the sites and at roadside vendors to find some archaeological replicas or other local handicrafts. We always like to bring back some replicas of artifacts from the sites we visit as reminders of our experiences. On this trip, it was a bit harder to find what we were looking for. One good place that we can recommend for a good selection of souvenirs is the booths at Tikal. Another is the town of Copán Ruinas in Honduras. Here we found a few shops selling souvenirs and mementos. We even found a decent selection from people right on the streets. Remember, haggling is the accepted way to complete these transactions.

Many sites in Guatemala are extremely remote, and the infrastructure to reach them has not been built up yet. Some are accessible only by boat or small plane. Most probably see not more than a handful of visitors each year, if that. The added challenge of getting to many of them adds to the adventure of it all. There is nothing like floating down a river on a tiny boat and arriving at an ancient site that appears suddenly out of dense, pristine jungle without any signs of modern civilization. In these areas, a strong sunblock and an effective insect repellent are essential for protection against the elements.

Other sites are easier to reach. For most there will be a small entrance fee, usually more for foreigners than for nationals. On a positive note, in Guatemala we were not charged any additional fees for using a video camera onsite, unlike sites in Mexico. We were pleased about this policy, since we were carrying two with us. Many of the sites are in thick rainforests and we struggled with rain on a near constant basis, even though we had consciously avoided the rainy season. So no matter when you go, some kind of rain gear is recommended. One of us had neglected to come prepared in this area and had to fashion a makeshift poncho out of a hastily appropriated garbage bag.

# The Adventure Begins

These ancient Mayan cities are truly amazing and well worth the effort to see them in person. Some of the most incredible achievements of the ancient world can be found here. Because of the remoteness of their locations, many sites have not been excavated much, and less has been put in place for tourism. The end result is that you can enter a site and have some impression of what the first modern explorers felt as they rediscovered these ancient wonders. In many cases, what we experienced was completely beyond what we had expected. Our successes and our setbacks came together to form a time that we will never forget. Even though things did not always go as planned, looking back at it all, we would not change a thing. Perhaps others can learn from what we went through, both the good and the bad. If you go, your experiences will be different from ours, but your life will be forever enriched by contact with this beautiful, ancient world.

# KAMINALJUYÚ

Stela 11

unexcavated mound

entrance to the excavations

## How We Got There

Many Mayan sites are located in remote areas surrounded by jungle or perhaps at the edge of towns that have sprung up near them. Kaminaljuyú is different in that it is completely surrounded by the suburbs of present-day Guatemala City. To get there, all you need to do is take a short ride by bus or taxi, so there is much less adventure involved than in reaching other sites. The payoff here is proportional to the amount of effort required, it seems. On the surface, neither the journey nor the site itself yields substance for great stories.

The capital city of Guatemala is divided into at least 17 zones, which serve as part of street addresses and help in getting around. Kaminaljuyú is in Zone 7. The only real significance this has is that you can you can say "zona siete" to a taxi driver if he has any question about where to go. You also may give the impression that you know what you are talking about.

We found a driver willing to take us to the site and then wait for us while we looked around. We really cannot describe the route he took, since much of Guatemala City is a maze of nondescript streets and run-down buildings. Our suspicion

## BACKGROUND

Unlike the rest of the sites we visited, Kaminaljuyú is truly a Preclassic site with an extremely long history, inhabited by at least 1000 BC.[1] Around 600 BC, it experienced a boom of growth and construction; the first of its irrigation canals being built during this era.[2] These canals connected to the nearby Lake Miraflores, which was an important source of water to the ancient city. Eventually, a network of canals was built to bring water to the fields, the longest one running at least two kilometers out from the lake.[3]

Kaminaljuyú was the largest city in the Preclassic Guatemalan Highlands and dominated the entire area.[4] Just building the canals required at least 10,000 workers.[5] Because of volcanic activity, the rich soils yielded good crops, and these valleys have been among the most densely populated in the Highlands.[6] A nearby source of obsidian, the "steel" of ancient America, ensured power and wealth for the leaders of Kaminaljuyú, and they came to dominate the trade routes in the precious resources of obsidian, cacao, and

*(continued on page 26)*

jade.[7] The results of this control of commerce can be seen in the tombs of Kaminaljuyú's Preclassic kings, whose burial caches, replete with pottery, masks, jade, obsidian, stingray spines, and quartz, rival those of the greatest Classic-era kings.[8]

Many characteristics once thought to be exclusive to the Classic era are now known to have existed at Kaminaljuyú centuries earlier. The carving of monumental stelae appeared here by 500 BC.[9] Some were as tall as six feet and included a simplified form of writing, but no Mayan Long Count dates. Themes of the carvings include a bearded god, Preclassic rulers with bound prisoners of war, and one of the longest Preclassic texts ever found.[10] The style of carving and imagery is known as Izapan, named for a nearby Preclassic site in Mexico. The stylistic similarity may indicate a cultural connection or exchange between these and other early sites near the Pacific coast. Other finds here, such as very fine ceramics and the use of pyramids as tombs for important individuals,[11] show that the Preclassic civilizations were just as highly developed as those of the later Classic, long considered the peak of Mayan culture. An

## BOOK OF MORMON COMPARISONS

*More than any other site we visited, Kaminaljuyú most likely has the closest connection to the Book of Mormon. Settlement here dates back to Jaredite times, but major periods of construction and agriculture occurred well after the arrival of Lehi's group. This site has figured prominently in some LDS authors' reconstructions of Book of Mormon geography. Our purpose is not to try and label sites definitively, but this is certainly one worth remembering. It is just frustrating that so much of its history is lost forever.*

## Right Time and Place

Kaminaljuyú's ancient origins offer a unique glimpse into the distant past of Mesoamerica. With other sites, Classic-era structures usually obliterated any trace of earlier settlement, but examples of art and architecture dating back to at least 500 BC have been found here. Its location relatively close to the Pacific coast, the commonly accepted location of Lehi's group's arrival, makes it a geographical fit as well. According to 2 Nephi 5:5–8, in about 550 BC Nephi took a group of loyal followers and fled from the rest of their group, thus creating the first division into Nephites and Lamanites. They traveled for many days (presumably inland) to establish a new settlement that was called Nephi. A city later identified as Lehi-Nephi was built, and all the features of a high level of civilization were developed, including permanent buildings, metallurgy, and agriculture. It was described as being "up" or higher in elevation from other lands.

Even though they disagree on the locations of some other sites, many LDS scholars

*(continued on page 27)*

that has been supported time and time again is that taxi drivers, both foreign and domestic, tend to take the longest and most circuitous way they can to get you to your destination. Whether this was the case with us we cannot say. We just know that it did feel a little strange to be taking a taxi through urban sprawl to visit an ancient site with so much history.

*Trying to find something interesting to look at*

early form of writing developed here by 400 BC, which brought about dramatic political changes extending north to the Lowlands.[12] In fact, it is currently believed that the initial source of many features considered typical of the later Mayan culture is to be found along the Pacific coast and Guatemalan Highlands. This is somewhat strange because sites in this region, including Kaminaljuyú, are considered atypical when compared to the rest of Mayan culture.[13]

Between 200 BC and AD 100, changes in climate dried up Lake Miraflores, rendering the irrigation system useless. A major change in procuring and storing water led to the use of wells, but this technique was apparently not as successful and Kaminaljuyú began to decline, eventually leading to a drop in population.[14] As the Classic era began, the city was left in ruins while sites in the Lowlands and Mexico were flourishing. One of these cities, Teotihuacán, played an important role in reviving Kaminaljuyú's lost splendor. It came

under control of this powerful Mexican city, either through occupation or invasion, which must not have been extremely difficult by this time. A hybrid of Mexican and Mayan cultures developed here, manifested in pottery styles and burial offerings.[15] Kaminaljuyú may have served as an outpost for rulers of Teotihuacán as they expanded their influence into the Petén. While Tikal was under this foreign influence, its Mexican ruler Curl Nose, who rose to power in AD 378, may have been from Kaminaljuyú.[16]

During this period of Mexican occupation, Kaminaljuyú's structures included hundreds of earthen mounds, some 66 feet high. Buildings of adobe and wood with thatched roofs were perched on top. Massive tomb complexes built of adobe were also built. Its foreign rulers even constructed a

(*Right Time and Place continued*) have picked Kaminaljuyú or its environs as a likely candidate for the land of Nephi.[24] This may be the case, although it should be remembered that Kaminaljuyú had already been inhabited for over 500 years by the time Nephi led his righteous followers away from their first settlement along the coast. We will never know for sure, but the land of Nephi and its associated cities could very well have been in the Valley of Guatemala. It is at a higher elevation than the coastal areas and the jungles to the north, with a desirable climate, making it perfect for settlements. All things considered, it does look like a good match. But did Nephi and his group join with an existing group of people or remain separate? This is another question that is hard to answer. It is interesting to note that according to the archaeological record, this area exerted a large amount of influence in the Preclassic era and appears to have been the source of many benchmarks of later Mayan culture. Writing, monumental architecture, and the carving of stelae were developed at Kaminaljuyú around the time that Nephi and his group settled in the land of Nephi. Is there a connection? The possibilities are intriguing.

Also interesting are the theories regarding Kaminaljuyú's late Preclassic collapse. It has been suggested that before this happened, the elite (and literate) class migrated away from Kaminaljuyú and settled elsewhere, perhaps in the Copán Valley, in present-day Honduras.[25] The Book of Mormon tells us in

(continued on page 29)

miniature version of Teotihuacán here.[17] But at the end of the Classic era, the city's prosperity waned again, this time for good. In the eighth century as Tikal declined and Teotihuacán was sacked and burned, Kaminaljuyú also fell into decline,[18] its fate now inextricably linked to these capitals of Mexican and Mayan culture. Although some habitation continued into the Postclassic era, it was abandoned by the time of the Spanish conquest.[19]

The first archaeological work here was done in the 1880s when Alfred Maudslay mapped more than 200 mounds. Manuel Gamio began the first excavations in 1925, discovering Preclassic artifacts. In 1935, a local soccer club found mounds with adobe structures and tombs while digging to expand their playing field. After this discovery, Alfred Kidder and Oliver Ricketson began new excavations here for the Carnegie Institute.[20] During this time Antonio Villacorta, the Minister of Public Education in Guatemala City, named the site Kaminaljuyú (sometimes split into Kaminal Juyú), which according to the sign at the site means "Hill of the Dead" in Quiché Maya, although we have also seen it translated as "Place of the Ancient Ones."[21] Its original name is not known. Excavations have continued here, some as recently as 2003. In June of 2007, Travis Doering and Lori Collins of the University of South Florida began scanning stelae and other items from the Popol Vuh Museum in Guatemala City as part of the Kaminaljuyú Sculpture Project. The data from these scans were turned into 3-D computer models for further study.

# BRIEF SITE OVERVIEW

At first glance, Kaminaljuyú looks more like a modern park than an ancient archaeological site. There is a large, grass-covered field with paths that meander around what seem to be small hills. Entrance to the park itself is free, so you will likely see people all around, relaxing and playing. Sadly, there is not much to see here; modern development has consumed about 90 percent of the ancient city. The same fate has befallen many sites in southern Guatemala,[22] so we may never have a clear understanding of this area's Preclassic history.

The hills are, of course, mounds from the ancient construction of the city. A path leading to the left takes you to a low structure with a corrugated roof, surrounded by chain-link fence. This was built to protect the structures that have been excavated. As we were peering through the locked gate, a caretaker approached and unlocked it for us. He did not ask for a fee, but this was on a Sunday when many sites can be visited free of charge. We do not know if it is usually locked, but we excitedly went in, grateful to be afforded a closer look at the oldest structure we had yet encountered in all our travels throughout Mesoamerica.

The difference in construction is immediately apparent. Unlike the other sites we visited, Kaminaljuyú's surviving structures were built of adobe, not stone. They also look plain and simple compared to the ornate façades of many later Mayan cities, but they could have been covered with stucco that has long since wasted away. To protect the earthen construction, narrow, wooden walkways lead from the gate to all the areas that are open to visitors. These structures are mostly below the current ground level. The surrounding earth and the protective roof overhead combine to block a lot of natural light from these structures, so a flashlight is useful here.

It is hard to distinguish many buildings from others, but we did see wide staircases, tunnels, large rooms, small chambers, and some expansive open areas. The best way to see it all is just to walk along the wooden walkways, following them to where they take you. The only identifying marks are some small signs identifying certain structures. If you find Structure E-III-3, you can look for its Burial C, which contained one of the richest Preclassic tombs. An important individual was interred here with an offering of over 300 artifacts. Also buried were four victims sacrificed for the occasion.[23] Sadly, there are no monuments, artifacts, or other decoration left at the site, so it looks quite bare. Everything that has been found has been taken to museums within the city. The artistry of the carvings is superb, so we recommend a visit to at least one of them as part of the Kaminaljuyú experience. The nearest one is the Miraflores

(Right Time and Place continued) Omni 12–15 that the prophet Mosiah led a righteous group away from the Land of Nephi to escape the wickedness there, probably in 121 BC. They went down from the higher elevations where they had been living to find a new area to settle. However, they apparently traveled north and eventually joined with the people living in the Land of Zarahemla who claimed to be descendants of Mulek, a son of the Jewish king Zedekiah. Copán is east of Kaminaljuyú and has never been suggested as a candidate for Zarahemla.

## Preclassic Writing

The elite at Kaminaljuyú were fully literate at a time when most of the Mayan world probably had no concept of writing.[26] An early form of writing was developed in the Guatemalan Highlands by 400 BC.[27] While this writing has not been deciphered, it has been suggested that these hieroglyphs were a special, elite language that is no longer spoken.[28] Remnants of what is probably the same written language have been found as near as Takalik Abaj on the Pacific coast and as far away as El Mirador in northern Guatemala,[29] both Preclassic sites. These hieroglyphs show some similarities to both the contemporary Epi-Olmec and the later Lowland Mayan writing systems,[30] but no definitive decision regarding how they fit into the evolution of ancient American writings has been reached.

This is because of the small number of characters that have been found so far. Stela

Museum, a short walk to the south of the site. It deals specifically with the history and artifacts of Kaminaljuyú. Other impressive stelae and carvings from excavations here can be found in the National Museum of Archaeology and the Popol Vuh Museum.

Since the fenced park area is only a fraction of the ancient site, there are still remnants scattered throughout other areas of the modern city. Across the street, we saw what appeared to be some small excavated structures covered and locked like the main structure within the park. Other mounds can be found elsewhere in Zone 7, as well as in Zones 3 and 11. As far as we know, they are still pristine and we do not know if there are plans for excavation.

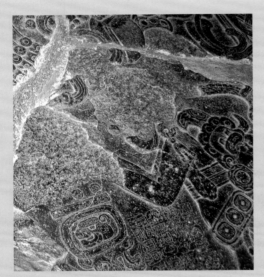

10 from Kaminaljuyú contains one of the longest known Preclassic texts, but it consists of only about 43 legible glyphs, some of which are repeated. Based on comparisons with other ancient writing systems, these probably represent less than 10 percent of the total characters for this written language.[31] What then, is the reason for the scarcity of such Preclassic texts? Obviously, some texts were written on perishable materials such as bark paper, wood, or leather that have not survived. Another answer comes from a turbulent period in Kaminaljuyú's history. At some point, possibly coinciding with its Preclassic collapse, all of the texts at Kaminaljuyú were intentionally and systematically defaced or destroyed, possibly by an invading force, making them illegible.[32] Were it not for this violent act of erasing history, we might have a greater knowledge of what took place in this formative area.

The Book of Mormon suggests that the same practices existed among the Lamanites. Their version of the contention between Laman and Nephi was understandably different from what was recorded on the plates. Although we know of no written records kept by the Lamanites, they did preserve an oral tradition of being robbed by the youngest brother for centuries. Nephi's nephew Enos writes in Enos 1:13–14, asking the Lord to preserve their records because the Lamanites already wanted to destroy them, along with all Nephite traditions. In Mormon 6:6, over 900 years later, Mormon hides up the records because the Lamanites were still trying to destroy them. Even after the complete destruction or

*Undeciphered text from Stela 10*

assimilation of the Nephite nation, the Lamanites continued to hunt down and kill any Nephite who would not deny Christ. Moroni, being one of these few faithful ones, had to constantly wander northward to keep himself and the records safe. Perhaps the Lamanites also knew that any surviving records would still be in the hands of a faithful Nephite, and were doing all they could to remove any contradictory account of their history.

Just understanding this drive to destroy writings helps to explain to critics why no golden plates engraved with reformed Egyptian have been found in Mesoamerica. The Book of Mormon itself explains that important Nephite records would have been well hidden (perhaps divinely protected) to keep them safe. Any that the Lamanites found would have been immediately destroyed. If some happened to survive until the Conquest, the Spanish in their lust for gold would have converted them into ingots, not caring for their historical or spiritual value. Even records that had no worth to them suffered. During his time in the Yucatán, Friar Diego de Landa destroyed thousands of carvings he considered idols and burned every book he could find, thinking that they were evil and were a hindrance to bringing Christianity to the natives. Because of his acts, only four Mayan codices exist today. Considering this trend of destroying unpopular writings described by Book of Mormon writers and attested by many periods of history, it is no wonder that Mesoamerica has yielded no written proof.

# Early Permanent Structures

It was quite a thrill for us to walk among buildings that dated back to early Book of Mormon times. In many ways, they were not as grand and magnificent as the ceremonial centers of the Classic Mayan cities, but that is to be expected. These were at least 1000 years older than most of the other buildings we explored in other Mayan areas. And since they were made of adobe and not stone, they could not be expected to last as long. Not many details are given in the Book of Mormon about construction techniques, but it is reasonable to expect that the Nephites would have used building methods with perishable materials requiring less manpower, at least at the beginning of their history. Many Preclassic structures, especially residential buildings, were made out of such materials as wood, adobe, and thatch that would not survive until our day. The well-known massive pyramids and decorated temples of stone were created by the Maya to represent aspects of their many gods and beliefs and to create a sense of awe among the people. It is likely that Nephites would not have had such needs, especially if they were truly living the commandments of God. We would expect their public and religions buildings to be much simpler and not have the same ornamentation as the Maya had.

# Agriculture

Feeding the population is an important consideration for any civilization, and permanent cities almost by definition require a successful system of agriculture, year after year. Every site we visited had to provide foodstuffs for its people, either directly or indirectly, through trade. We make particular mention of it at Kaminaljuyú because of the effort they put into building at least three canals for irrigation, but what we found here could apply to most ancient sites.

Corn, beans, and squash are commonly known as the staples of the ancient American diet. Some books may suggest that the canals brought water to maize fields, but because the cooler climate in the valley of Guatemala provided plenty of precipitation for growing corn, the fields fed by the canals must have been for some other crop.[33] It is known that other crops besides the big three were cultivated, but our understanding of Mayan agriculture is incomplete. For years, archaeologists have suspected that the Maya grew manioc, or cassava, for its high energy value, but there has been no proof of it until recently. In August of 2007, the University of Colorado at Boulder announced that its archaeological team under Payson Sheets had discovered a manioc field in the ancient Mayan village of Cerén in El Salvador.[34] The field had been buried and perfectly preserved under 10 feet of ash by a volcanic eruption around AD 600. Although this is the only example of ancient cultivated manioc found, Sheets hopes to find more such fields in the region.

Finding evidence of Book of Mormon agriculture has been somewhat tricky. It is obvious that most, if not all, groups mentioned in it raised some kind of crops. Second Nephi 5:11, Enos 21, and Mosiah 9:9 specifically state that the Nephites sowed seed, tilled the ground, and harvested. The only recognizable crops ever recorded are corn, wheat, and barley. Corn is no surprise, having been an American staple since archaic times, but it is significant that when referring to fields or harvests, Book of Mormon writers refer to corn more often than any other crop and whenever more than one grain is mentioned, corn always comes first. This fits in with the major role that maize played in all aspects of Mesoamerican life.

Barley and wheat are a different issue, long believed to be crops native to the Old World. But it is now known that the Hohokam, an ancient culture from what is now Arizona, included an American form of barley as a regular part of their diet long before Europeans arrived.[35] This good source of sugar, carbohydrates, and plant proteins is also known as "little barley" or "barley grass" and may have been cultivated in addition to having been gathered in the wild. There is at present no strong evidence for wheat in pre-Columbian America, but it should be remembered that the Book of Mormon only mentions it once, in about 190 BC. The recent surprise of the Manioc fields at Cerén should be an example that the intervening millennia have hidden much of ancient history and there is still a lot out there that has not been discovered yet.

# THE ARCHAEOLOGICAL MUSEUM IN GUATEMALA CITY

The national archaeological museum, or Museo Nacional de Arqueología y Etnología, is located in Zone 13, just down the street from the zoo and almost within walking distance from the airport. Across the parking lot from it is the modern art museum, but our interests at this time lay solely in the most ancient forms of Guatemalan artwork. We paid the nominal fee at the front desk and began our tour. For a major state-run museum, it is a little small and antiquated, but the collection of exhibits is impressive. We realize that reading about a museum may not be very exciting, so we will just give a brief description and point out some things to look for. We definitely recommend a visit here to supplement the site of Kaminaljuyú so you can get a more accurate idea of the splendor of ancient Mayan civilization.

*See, Nephites and Lamanites **can** get along.*

In the main hall near the entrance to the exhibits is a nice reproduction of a Classic Mayan mural, showing two individuals with very different skin color. We realize that traditional archaeologists would probably explain this as a symbolic use of body paint, but we have always found representations like this interesting and feel that there is more to the story. For a discussion on the apparent ethnic diversity shown in ancient Mayan art, see the chapter on Bonampak.

*Now this was unexpected.*

The exhibits are divided into Preclassic, Classic, and Postclassic, which will help you to understand the age of what you are looking at and get a feel for the development of Mayan culture. The many examples of pottery and ceramics are interesting, but we were struck by a small object included in this section that was simply labeled as a carved piece of shell. The image was unmistakably a Star of David, and the fact that it was from Book of Mormon times brings many questions to mind. We would love to know more about this piece, such as where it was found, if it can be conclusively dated, and what a conventional explanation of it might be. At this

point, these questions remain unanswered.

The Classic section contains items that most people would associate with the Mayan culture. We quite enjoyed the model of Tikal at the peak of its power. Not to be missed is the wooden lintel taken from one of its major temples. Even from behind the glass, its superior craftsmanship and minute detail can be appreciated. We were reminded of John L. Stephens's assertion that these very hard woods must have been carved with metal tools. A few examples of such tools are here in this section, which has a small display of copper items, including some ax heads. Some impressive stone and wood weapons of war are worth a glance too.

Occupying a central spot in the museum is its wide-ranging assortment of stelae, obviously the pride of its collections. These range from Preclassic examples taken from nearby Kaminaljuyú to others carved perhaps 1000 years later from Piedras Negras, an extremely remote site in the northern jungles bordering Mexico. Much to our surprise, we found an *utiya* glyph meaning "It came to pass" as we were looking at one of them. The ornate throne carved for a Classic-era king in this section was worth seeing as well.

The last part of the tour is the modern section, which includes artifacts and products from the

*Look, twin body-building missionaries!*

Spanish Conquest up to the modern day. A nice collection of textiles and traditional costumes can be found here. Near the exit, a mural high on the wall represents additional religious influences in Guatemala since the introduction of Catholicism. Among the images are two blond, very muscular, almost Aryan-looking young men, wearing ties and white shirts. These are, of course, LDS missionaries, each carrying a blue book. The stereotype is regrettable, but at least we were granted a place in their religious history.

Our schedule did not permit much time in the city for looking around, but if time permits, we do recommend a visit to the Popol Vuh Museum in Zone 10. It also has a nice collection of stelae and monuments and was the site of a project that began in the summer of 2007 by scientists from the University of South Florida to scan them and convert the data into 3-D computer models for further study. There is also the Miraflores Museum just to the south of Kaminaljuyú, which is dedicated to the history and artifacts from that ancient site.

# THE PACAYA VOLCANO

There are over 30 volcanoes in Guatemala formed by the subduction of the Cocos Plate underneath the Caribbean Plate. It is quite impressive to see many of these massive cones rising up above the city of Guatemala. Since 1965, Pacaya has been continuously active with eruptions that range from minor gas and steam emissions to explosions that can hurl rock up to seven miles and cause evacuations of nearby villages. In a region that has seen a lot of volcanic activity, Pacaya is one of the most active. We were excited at the prospect of reaching its summit to see just what kind of volcanic activity we would find.

On the way out of the city we made a quick stop at a small grocery store along the main road. After stocking up with fruit, snacks, and several gallons of water and making another failed ATM attempt, we were on our way. The wide, modern highway of CA 9 was easy to follow, and we headed south toward Esquintla until we came to the turnoff for San Vicente Pacaya. Here we continued west toward the small town of San Francisco de Sales, driving up narrow, dirt switchbacks that took us into the jungle hills. As we found with almost every city in Guatemala, there are not many signs showing the way. Nearing the town, we stopped to ask directions to the volcano. A man indicated that we were on the right road and offered to guide us up to the volcano.

We declined, feeling that a guide was not needed, but we must mention that we were somewhat nervous about climbing the volcano. Guidebooks and travel websites mentioned trouble with being held up, robbed, and sometimes even injured by thieves along the way. Machetes were commonly used by the thieves and some tourists hiking the volcanoes had been attacked as they tried to escape. A particularly sinister tactic employed against hikers was for a so-called guide to lead them along the trail to the volcano, only to disappear later at a spot where his armed

cohorts were waiting to ambush and rob the foreign tourists. This was not our experience, and it seems things have changed over the last couple of years as government patrols and law enforcement have basically eradicated the problem. With these stories in mind, we did not even consider hiring a guide, but we need not have been so concerned. First of all, the trails are easy to follow, and second, there were many people about, including families and young people. It was a very casual, safe setting.

There are two trails that lead to the top of the volcano. The more commonly used trail starts at San Francisco de Sales, and the second starts at the complex of radio towers on the flank of Cerro Chino. We stuck with the main trail since we were already there. Across the street from the bottom of the trailhead was a small parking lot. An elderly woman who apparently lived nearby was hanging around it and we made an agreement with her to watch our car while we were gone. We got the impression that this was one of her occupations. Shortly after starting the trail, we came to the official entrance, which serves as a place to pay and gain access to the national park. We had a clear day for the hike which paid off with rewarding views of the volcanoes de Fuego and de Agua to the west. The trail was dusty and steep. Occasionally,

## BOOK OF MORMON COMPARISONS

## Quaking of the Earth

Our experience at the top of the Pacaya Volcano showed us just how seismically active this region can be. The surrounding volcanoes, mostly dormant, also serve as mute witnesses to the violent activity that must have occurred here in the past. The southern Highlands of Guatemala are still plagued with frequent volcanic eruptions and earthquakes.[1] This geologic activity has been a major force in the area for thousands of years. Settlements as far back as the Preclassic period were affected by volcanoes and other natural disasters. Payson Sheets of the University of Colorado believes that volcanic eruptions and their resulting lava flows destroyed many late Preclassic settlements in the Guatemalan Highlands.[2] If the destruction was widespread enough, it may have been a factor in the demise of many Preclassic sites.[3]

There is evidence of unrepaired earthquake damage at Xunantunich, a site in the central Lowlands. Other sites in this area that comprises northern Guatemala and the southern Yucatán Peninsula were abandoned.[4] Occupation at some sites came to a sudden dramatic end in various locations throughout Mesoamerica. Between 585 and AD 600, the town of Cerén in what is now El Salvador was buried under 15 feet of volcanic ash.[5] Also in El Salvador, the Ilopango

(continued on page 39)

37

hikers on foot and some on horseback passed us coming down from the volcano, which could not be seen for most of the climb. Periodically we passed small booths along the trail where locals were selling drinks and snacks. Keeping hydrated was a necessity along the way because the day was hot and muggy. We paused many times to catch our breath, wishing we had prepared more for the physical demands of the day. It is a gradual climb to reach the open area at the base of the cone where the lava fields start. Reaching this point takes two to three grueling hours. It is marked by a sign in Spanish, translated into English, that warned us we would be "exposed to harmful gases to [our] health and fall of rocks that may cause [us] serious consequences."

Rather than stick to the trail off to the side, we opted for the slower and more precarious route up the lava fields. Although going this way seemed more direct, it was probably longer and more difficult because of the jagged and uneven landscape. However, it did provide for some unexpected entertainment. As we got closer to the volcano, we came across vents or cracks in the lava that were encrusted with white minerals. Intense heat could be felt streaming out of them. We found what looked like small limes on the ground and decided to drop them down these crevices. Almost immediately, they began to hiss and then exploded from the heat. When we found discarded garbage (not our own), we tried the same thing. The bits of paper or wrappers burst into flames right away. After an hour or so of fun and exertion, we made our way back to the trail. The last part of the hike was the most strenuous. The angle of the final ascent up the slippery slope of sand and loose volcanic rock to the cone increased dramatically. For every step we took, we slid back halfway.

As we neared the summit, we began to hear and feel belching from deep within the volcano, sounding like distant bass drums rumbling madly. Once we reached the summit, we saw that the rumbling was accompanied by blasts of steam and vapor escaping from fissures in the ground. From a distance, what looked to be wispy clouds floating atop the volcano turned out to be an endless haze of noxious sulfuric fumes. It was so dense that we could not see much of the top of the volcano; we just stayed near the edge where the heat and fumes were less intense. Most of the time, we were able to breathe without problems, but every so often the wind blew an unavoidable cloud of steam that sent us coughing and gasping for breath. It was an intense experience, to say the least. The ground was warm beneath our feet and shook from time to time with the rumbling. Yellow sulfur stained much of the rock and soil, especially around openings in the ground. This may sound like an incredibly dangerous situation, but since there were around ten other people (locals

and tourists) on top with us, we felt fairly safe.

At a distance we estimated to be 60 to 70 feet from where we were standing, two cones rose from the summit. Every so often in addition to the steam being vented all over the place, we noticed material being thrown up from the smaller of the cones. It was quite active and as our eyes adjusted to our surroundings, we were amazed to see that it was bright orange lava being thrown out. Once the lava shot over fifty feet in the air and sent us running for cover, not that there was any to be found. Being so close to this natural show of the earth's raw power was unbelievable, and we were amazed it was even allowed. It was a must-see and a great way to start our day! Facing away from the clouds of sulfur, we took in the incredible panorama of the highlands all around that included views of several other volcanoes and Guatemala City.

(Quaking of the Earth continued) volcano erupted around AD 175, bringing widespread destruction and covering the Zapotitan Valley in three feet of ash, rendering a 100-km radius that included the site of Chalchuapa uninhabitable for over a century.[6] Earlier, the site of Cuicuilco in central Mexico was buried by volcanic eruptions by AD 100.[7]

The Book of Mormon describes cataclysmic geologic events that took place at the time of the Savior's death, presumably around AD 33. These upheavals were so severe that they destroyed many cities and changed the face of the land. Third Nephi chapter 8 gives an account of the storms, fires, and other disasters that wreaked havoc at this time. In verse 10, the city of Moronihah is covered by earth so that a mountain appeared in the place of the city. This certainly sounds like a description of a cataclysmic volcanic eruption. Verses 12 and 13 describe that in the land northward, storms and earthquakes were so intense that roads and highways were broken up and the whole face of the land was changed. According to verses 14 and 15, many cities were sunk and others were shaken so that buildings fell to the ground. Again, this sounds like a description of the results of lava and pyroclastic flows and earthquakes. It is even possible that the vapor of darkness mentioned in verse 20 that extinguished all light was caused by falling ash from nearby volcanic eruptions.

The understanding of the history of Preclassic sites is incomplete, but it is known that
(continued on page 41)

In comparison to the ascent, the hike down the volcano was quick and easy. The loose ground below proved to make a fast descent down the cone. We were glad to see our vehicle in place and gear seemingly untouched, so we thanked our "guard." Once again, we had a difficult time finding our way out of town and to the highway. We stopped a few times to get directions out of the steep, twisty roads, trying to interpret the vague information we received. Once back on the main highway, we had to decide which way to go. Our goal was to reach Antigua, the provincial capital of Guatemala, for dinner. Hoping to save some time, we continued on the road to Esquintla, noticing a turnoff to Antigua on our map. We traveled south on CA 9 for longer than we expected, but eventually we arrived at the turn to Antigua, just before the town of Palín. After more than an hour, and being diverted through a detour of back streets, we arrived in Antigua, a beautiful city famous for its colonial architecture that is a favorite tourist destination. It lies within the shadow of two large volcanoes, probably the same ones we had seen on our hike up Pacaya.

We pulled into the main plaza as the sun was setting. The center of town was full of people and activity. Spying some open spots on a curb by an arched colonnaded building across the street from the plaza, we pulled up and asked two soldiers patrolling the area if it was okay for us to park there. They replied that it was. Pleased with our good fortune, we got out and strolled around the plaza, visited the local Catholic church, and found a great restaurant a few blocks away. By this

time we were sore, hungry, and tired, and all we cared about was a filling meal. We barely noticed that we were still covered in ash and dust from the volcano.

After a delicious and satisfying meal, we returned to the plaza for a rude awakening: a locking boot had been attached to one of our wheels! It turns out that we were in a no parking zone after all. We asked around and were directed to an office to pay a fine. We tried to protest, saying that the

soldiers had approved of it, but the attendant would not budge. The fine turned out to be 250 quetzals. We had to pay it and then return to our vehicle to wait for someone to come by and unlock us. While we were waiting, we struck up a conversation with an irate local who had been booted as well. He ran a tour agency and had asked a policeman if he could park there while he ran into the church for mass. Having been given permission, he did so and returned to find himself in the same predicament as us. The whole thing sounded like a scam. So our advice is, do not park along the main plaza, no matter what someone in authority tells you!

*This is what we get for listening to local law enforcement.*

(*Quaking of the Earth continued*) natural disasters such as eruptions and earthquakes played a part in Mesoamerica's past. It is important to note that the demise of settlements due to geologic forces is believed to have taken place in the late Preclassic era, a period of time that corresponds with Book of Mormon chronology for its own destructive events. The fact that areas identified as likely candidates for Book of Mormon sites are within regions of volcanic and earthquake activity is worthy of note as well. It is unlikely that Joseph Smith would have known so much about Central American geography.

These events are still occurring. Pacaya has been erupting almost continuously for decades. As recently as 2005, lava has flowed out and down its sides. Away from the immediate vicinity of volcanoes, Guatemala City has also suffered movements of the earth. In February of 2007, a large sinkhole opened up, swallowing part of a residential neighborhood. It is thought that rainstorms may have been part of the cause for the ground giving way.[8] It is interesting that 3 Nephi 8:5-6 describes fierce storms and tempests that preceded the destruction of many cities, some of which were sunk and buried in the ground.

We had reserved a hotel room in the town of Panajachel, on the shores of Lake Atitlán. It was already night, so we were anxious to get there. We took CA 1 out of Antigua and headed north. On the map it did not look far, but soon we were climbing narrow, curvy mountain passes with precipitous drop-offs. To make matters worse, a thick fog rolled in, bringing visibility down to almost nothing. Somewhere near the peak of these mountains, we arrived at a three-way intersection. Turning left, we soon took the road to Sololá, a town just before Panajachel. Now we were descending rapidly, having crested the lip of an ancient volcanic caldera, the bottom of which held the lake.

We quickly drove through Sololá and entered Panajachel (often just called Pana). By now it was 10:00 in the evening, but the town was very quiet and most places looked closed. We had previously made a reservation at a reasonable hotel not far from the shore, the Posada Monterosa. Turning down a narrow unlit street, we arrived at what we believed was the correct address, but we could not see a light on anywhere. We got out and rang the buzzer at the gate. Shortly, someone answered and we told him that we were here. To our astonishment, he seemed not to know who we were and said there were no vacancies. Another night of this was just too much! This time, we knew we had the right place and that the reservation had definitely been made. A few minutes of arguing convinced him of this and he finally opened the gate and let us drive into the courtyard. Obviously, this was not the guy we made reservations with.

Having a secure parking area was a relief and one of the reasons we had picked this hotel. The three-bed room was simple but clean and met our needs, the first of which was to get cleaned up from the adventures of the day. A few nice hot showers later and we felt good as new, except for being completely exhausted. We went to bed early in anticipation of the long day we expected the following day. It turned out to be much more than we ever could have expected.

# Lake Atitlán

Lake Atitlán is one of the most beautiful places we visited in Guatemala, and that says a lot. This pristine lake fills the remains of an ancient volcanic caldera in the southwestern region of Guatemala and is close to 1,000 feet deep. There have been several recent volcanoes that have formed along the shores, creating a beautiful vista of mountains along the shoreline. The geography is breathtaking and explains why this is the most popular tourist destination in Guatemala.

We spent the night in Panajachel at the Posada Monterosa close to the lake. Early in the morning we climbed to the top of the hotel to take in the incredible panorama. Rooftop access is a common feature of many buildings in this area. The morning was clear and the air crisp as we looked across the water to the stunning volcanoes framing the lake. The water was smooth and calm, mirroring the volcanoes all around.

We checked out from our hotel, loaded up, and headed down to the shore of the lake. Since it was still early in the morning, we were the only ones around and were amazed at the peaceful, quiet shores. Although there were restaurants and stores along the shore, none of them had yet opened. This is a place we would have enjoyed staying for a while.

After leaving the shore, we headed for the center the of city, where small stores that lined the roads were beginning to open up, revealing the activity we had missed earlier. After seeing all kinds of food for sale, we went with bread and other baked goods. Then we saw a street vendor selling freshly squeezed orange juice. Concerned about the hygiene of the situation, but tempted by the prospect of such a refreshing drink for breakfast, we decided to take a chance. However,

only the bravest of us took the plunge, verifying it was safe and really orange juice, while the others watched. We are happy to report no negative effects and that the juice was delicious.

Unfortunately, we were in a rush to make our way north to Bethel. Had we had more time, we would have liked to cross the lake and visit Santiago Atitlán. This village sits on the southwest corner of the lake inside a small inlet right below the volcanoes. It serves as the largest and most important village along the lake and home to the Tzutujil-speaking Maya. Although the city is much more industrial now, it has retained much of its traditional grandeur in a unique setting. According to guidebooks, it is easily accessible by boat from Panajachel for a few dollars.

The road in and out of Panajachel is steep and curvy. Driving carefully, we slowly made our way out of the old crater and back into the highlands. On our way out we stopped at several small stands selling jewelry on the side of the road. This was another good opportunity to enjoy the spectacular views of the lake, but from a higher elevation. At the roadside stands, we selected some silver and jade jewelry and went through the obligatory process of haggling the prices down. This idyllic setting above the lake was perfect for spending some time chatting with the locals while beautiful young children played and posed for photographs. Our mission accomplished, we headed out and quickly made our way up to the main highway, luckily avoiding any accidents. Up to this point, we had enjoyed relatively good roads and were pleased to be making such good time. But our good fortune was about to change.

## BOOK OF MORMON COMPARISONS

## Fountain of Pure Water

The Guatemalan Highlands have been inhabited since very ancient times, even before the arrival of Lehi's group. The resources offered by Lake Atitlán and its environs would surely have attracted settlers. In fact, although it has been hard to find much information, archaeological work has been done at pre-Columbian sites on its shores. A few of these date back to the Preclassic and early Classic eras, including Chukumuk, Xikomuk, Tzanchicham, and Tolimán.[1] It should go without saying that not much has been widely published about these sites and they probably see few, if any, visitors. It is likely that more from the ancient record may lie under the surface of the lake, as some underwater archaeological work has been done.

Lake Atitlán is considered by notable LDS scholars and authors to be a strong candidate for the Waters of Mormon.[2] If the Land of Nephi was somewhere around the Valley of Guatemala, then it certainly is possible. In Mosiah 18:4–5, Alma leaves the city and hides in a thicket in a bordering region called Mormon. Near the thicket of trees was a fountain of pure water, or fresh water, as we would probably call it. The land was large enough and had enough cover so that Alma (and later his followers) could successfully hide from the forces of King Noah. The body of water was large enough to allow for the

many baptisms into the Church, as well as to provide for the needs of those early converts.

Eventually, about 450 people joined Alma in the Land of Mormon. Not only were the land and waters called Mormon, but verse 30 refers to the Forest of Mormon. There is certainly enough land and forests around Lake Atitlán to support such a number. In Mosiah 23:3–5, Alma is warned of approaching armies from King Noah and flees with his people into the wilderness. After eight days, they arrive at a beautiful and pleasant land of pure water. Here the people make what seems to be a permanent settlement, even constructing buildings and tilling fields. They call this land and their city within it Helam. Could this land have been on the shores of Lake Atitlán? The truth is that the lake is large enough that it could suffice for both areas. There are many inlets and secluded areas to provide cover for baptizing and hiding. If Alma and his people settled near a shore on the far end of the lake from the Land of Lehi-Nephi, they could have been far enough away to feel secure in building the city of Helam.

There is not much to do here now except enjoy the beauty of the lake and perhaps take in a few watersports. For those wishing to investigate the matter further, a boat ride across the lake to the town of Santiago Atitlán would be a good place to start. There are ancient sites in that area and you may be able to get some more information or a guide to take you there. Because of the lake's likely spot in Book of Mormon geography and the presence of Preclassic ruins dating to the correct time period near its shores, we feel that additional visits are warranted.

*Could this be near the site of Alma's baptisms?*

# Submerged City

The existence of ancient sites on the far side of Lake Atitlán dating back to Book of Mormon times is intriguing, but we have been unable to find out any more details about them. Apparently, most archaeological work done in this area has not been published outside of Guatemala, but we knew that Mayan artifacts had been recovered from the lake bottom. As of 2001, over 400 complete pieces and many other fragments were displayed in public and private collections.[3] Unknown to us at the time, many of these artifacts are on display at the Museo Lacustre de Atitlán, located in the upscale Posada de Don Rodrigo hotel, right in Panajachel. None of our guidebooks mentioned this collection, but it can be viewed every day from 8:00 a.m. to 5:00 p.m.

Artifacts dating from the Spanish conquest back to Preclassic times have also been found in other lakes in Guatemala, like Amatitlán and Petén Itzá.[4] So, how did they all get to the bottom of these lakes? A likely answer is that many were cast into the waters as part of religious ceremonies or offerings to the gods. We know that sacrifices of people and objects were found at the bottom of the sacred cenote at Chichén Itzá, which was viewed as an entrance to the underworld of Xibalba. Perhaps the same practice existed at Guatemalan lakes.

On land, artifacts are usually a sign of habitation. Could it be that in ancient times, water levels of the lakes were lower and that undiscovered cities lie submerged in their depths? The truth is that no underwater cities are mentioned in any scholarly literature or books by archaeologists that we could find. But in 1997, a diver named Roberto Samayoa discovered a small site at a depth of 15 meters. Built on a hill rising up from the floor of Lake Atitlán, he found walls, other structures, and artifacts within a 200 meter radius.[5] He dubbed this Postclassic site Samabaj. This discovery was presented at an archaeological symposium in Guatemala in 1999.

In his map of Book of Mormon geography, John Sorenson places the cities of Jerusalem and Ani-Anti on the southern shore of Lake Atitlán, identified as the Waters of Mormon. Since Jerusalem was covered by water at the time of the Savior's crucifixion, the suggestion is that the ancient city of Jerusalem now lies under the waters of the lake.[6] While the artifacts and especially the submerged site are tantalizing, we must point out that these finds are not old enough to be directly connected to the Book of Mormon. There are Preclassic sites near the shore in these areas, but they are still on land; none are underwater. The city of Jerusalem has not been located, and the newly found Samabaj cannot be a Book of Mormon city. But taken all together, what has been found around and in Lake Atitlán is promising, and the region deserves more study.

# Getting There: The Guatemala/Mexico Border

To say that this day did not turn out as we had planned would be an understatement. When it was all said and done, our response to the many things we experienced this day would have to be that we could not believe what just happened. The original goal was to get from one end of the country to the other as quickly and efficiently as we could and perhaps be at Yaxchilán by the afternoon. What we got was a 15-hour ordeal filled with multiple events that seemed so unexpected and bizarre that we just could not believe they kept occurring. The only upside is that (hopefully) they make for a good story.

It all started the morning we left Lake Atitlán on our way to Co-op Bethel. This was to be our longest driving leg of the trip. While planning our route, we were advised to return to Guatemala City and from there head north to Cobán, which serves as a gateway to the Petén jungle. Not wanting to double back, we decided to take what appeared to be the shorter route and travel through the western edge of the country through smaller towns. The roads on our map looked major enough. This decision provided a surprising and initially enjoyable drive that turned out to be not the most time efficient, to say the least. If you are short on time and patience, you may want to stay with the main roads and avoid some of the holdups we encountered. Although we took the slow route, it gave us a view into several remote areas of the country and a glimpse of Guatemala that few tourists see.

After stopping to buy local jewelry at a stand along the road, we headed north to Route CA-1. Instead of turning east and following it back to Guatemala City, we continued north on what became Highway 15. This road took us through several small towns and we got a good sense of what the country is really like.

We got momentarily turned around on the one-way streets in these small towns, crossed gorges on small suspension bridges, and got to see the landscape gradually change as we progressed farther northward. Just outside of a town where we had lunch, we came to a sudden halt as the cars became backed up in front of us. Up ahead, a flagman was blocking the road. We quickly learned that there was road construction up ahead and traffic would be stopped for an hour. After at

least an hour of sitting, walking, visiting with locals, and eating fruit sold along the side of the road, we were back on our way. It was at this point that we realized we might be in for a long day and that our effortless journey was proving anything but. As we learned, you just never know what to expect when you take the road less traveled.

With the delay of the road closure behind us, we thought we had seen it all and that things would improve. We were wrong; our delays were just beginning. The paved road soon deteriorated into a rough dirt trail as we entered a more mountainous region. We were stopped several

more times to wait for construction, but thankfully, not as long as the first time. As we were making our way along the rugged mountainside of a narrow canyon, we stopped by two pickup trucks parked in the road. We barely had time to wonder what was going on, for seconds later we heard loud explosions and were amazed to see clouds of dust and debris erupting from the cliffs ahead, sending a landslide of dirt, rocks, and large boulders falling down to the road in front of us. After two or three more such explosions, the road just around the bend was rendered completely impassible. This looked to be an insurmountable problem, for there was no way around the boulders that blocked the way of our nice little mountainside road. At this point, we did not know what to expect next. We were amazed

there were no signs or flagmen warning of the explosions and falling rock. Had we arrived a few moments earlier and passed the parked trucks, which we considered doing, we might have really needed the insurance we took out on our rented SUV (and maybe even a tow truck and an ambulance).

Stunned, we wondered if we would have to turn back and retrace our route, not seeing any way to drive through the debris on the road. But as soon as the dust had settled, two men came out from the side of the road and began pushing boulders out of the way to clear a path. We then noticed a worker who had set the charges descending the cliffs on a rope. Two of us watched as the other joined the local workers in manually removing the rocks from the road. Although this unusual delay was further hindering our progress, it was enjoyed afterward and provided laughs along the rest of the way.

The explosions were soon followed by a downpour of rain that quickly turned the dirt road into a slick muddy path. We were now in the Cuchumatanes Mountains, going up and down through dense jungle hills. The road was basically nonexistent or being built as we drove by. We saw plenty of dump trucks, cranes, and other machinery as construction workers were busy building the road that was already on our map. By now, we were grateful for the four-wheel drive capabilities of our Mitsubishi, since we would not have been able to make it through otherwise. The tension was heightened by the fact that we faced oncoming traffic from time to time along this narrow, muddy trail. The highlight of our trek came as we passed a large oncoming truck on the slippery hillside with a sheer drop-off to the right and almost no room to the left. As the truck edged

closer and squeezed past, we barely avoided being pushed off the edge as our driver reacquainted himself with the manual transmission. Needless to say, it was an intense moment. For most of the way, we kept our eyes on a blue cargo truck ahead of us. The driver seemed very confident on this jungle trail and was able to take shortcuts to bypass slow traffic and other problems. We followed him as closely as we could, hoping to be led out of this mess.

*Just keep following the blue truck and everything will be okay.*

Eventually the mud turned into gravel, which later became asphalt. We were approaching civilization once again! Honestly, we had become quite worried as to where we would emerge (if ever) from the Cuchumatanes. But late in the afternoon, we arrived in Cobán, a relatively large modern city. Parking along the main street, we ate a delicious dinner at an open-air taco shop along the road. After our satisfying meal, we visited a mall across the street. It was a surprise to see such modern facilities after having driven through so many small primitive villages. It looked like any upscale mall you would see in the United States. We had definitely seen the extremes of Guatemala today. Inside the mall, we went to a bank to get cash, bought supplies at a grocery store, and spent time in a bookstore on the Internet to send email back home. We ended up spending more time than we had anticipated; it was dark by the time we were out and back on our way. So much for seeing Yaxchilán that day.

We took Highway 5 and headed north into the Petén jungle, the most remote and unpopulated area in Guatemala. We were in completely new territory, but the road was good, so we kept the high beams on and drove fast to make up for the late hour. We had been told it would take us four hours to get there, but it ended up taking us eight. Now we realized that returning to Guatemala City and then driving to Cobán would have been the smart thing to do and would have saved us those four hours. But then, where would the fun in that be? Although we did not appreciate our trials and adventures at the time, they did make this day much more memorable and exciting, especially when recalled from the comfort of our own homes. At least now we know what to do next time.

There was practically no artificial lighting for the road, so we had to depend solely on our headlights to light our way through the dense jungle darkness. The road was direct and we encountered no problems, so we were making good time by this point. Our one snag was a detour of traffic cones, leading us off the road to a military checkpoint. A group of soldiers came out, questioned us about our destination, and inspected our vehicle. We had to allow them to do this, and entertained ourselves by watching fireflies buzzing around, illuminating the night with their tiny greenish-yellow lamps. To our surprise, the inspection turned up a few contraband items: produce we had purchased earlier that was immediately confiscated. The Petén must have suffered from attacks by vicious fruit.

Counting ourselves lucky, we got back on the road and continued the journey. It was not long before we passed the turnoff to the ancient site of El Ceibal. This would have been a nice place to visit, but it was now hours past closing time. If we had made better decisions earlier in the day, we might have been able to stop in for a quick look around.

At about 10:00 in the evening, we came to the town of Sayaxché. Once again, we found ourselves unsuccessfully trying to make our way out of a town. This time, we knew we needed to cross the San Martín River here but could not find a bridge to do so. Every street we took dead-ended at

*Well, this is one way to cross a river.*

the river without any visible way across. After turning around and looking for some time, we asked several locals who all replied that we needed to take the ferry to cross the river. Because it was so late and the people we were talking to seemed somewhat questionable in their judgment, we were more than a little skeptical. Finally, we returned to the river, drove down a gravel incline, and saw a small floating platform moored at the water's edge. This must be the "ferry" they were talking about. With a bit of trepidation, we drove onto the platform and two men appeared out of nowhere to get us across. Because of the lateness of the hour, the fare was a little more than it is during the day. It only amounted to a few dollars, so we happily paid them and they started up two small outboard motors and we slowly made our way across the water to the far side of the river. There, they lowered a ramp on that side of the "ferry" and we drove off and up a dirt hill. We soon found the paved road and were on our way once more.

A mere 13 kilometers past Sayaxché, we arrived at the turnoff to Bethel on the left. We took it, excited that we were getting closer to our destination. For about 80 kilometers, the road was paved and well maintained, taking us through the town of Las Cruces. When the pavement ended, we continued on a rough, rutted, dirt road, dodging rocks and holes for another 70 kilometers all the way into Co-op Bethel. It was midnight when we arrived, and our day had lasted 15 hours. Relieved to finally be there, we looked around and saw houses and buildings, but there was not a light on or a person out anywhere. The entire town had apparently closed down for the night. We would soon realize that this is commonplace in the Petén. But our surprises were not over yet. When we looked for the inn where we had planned to stay, we were in for one more shock.

# YAXCHILÁN

Structure 40

Bird Jaguar IV's head

"And then it came to pass."

## How We Got There

After our exhausting 15-hour day that started in Panajachel, we finally arrived at Co-op Bethel around midnight. Our guidebooks had mentioned that there was a hotel in town, the Posada Maya, so we were trying to head straight for it in the darkness. Much to our surprise, we could not find it anywhere, despite seeing a sign for it on the edge of town. We continued on the dirt road into town looking, without success, for another inn or someplace where we could spend the night. Not only were accommodations lacking, but everything was dark and quiet; there was no light, sound, nor anyone awake anywhere. We later discovered that at remote settlements in the jungles of northern Guatemala, the power is turned out at night and there is nothing to do but sleep until the dawn.

For the first time on our trip we decided it was time to use our camping gear. Finding a nearby open field, we set up camp. As soon as we took our tents out of the bags, it began raining. We worked fast and hard as the amount of rain increased. As quickly as possible, we had our tents erected and sleeping bags ready so we could finally try to fall asleep, waking up from time to time to the dripping in our tents and unknown animal sounds.

54 (continued on page 56)

## BACKGROUND

The original name of Yaxchilán was Siyankan or Sian-Chan.[1] Based on ceramics found there, it was possibly inhabited as early as 300 BC.[2] The early history of Yaxchilán is relatively unknown, but the dynastic history probably starts AD 359 with Yoaat Balam,[3] whose line continued unbroken until Yaxchilán's early ninth century collapse. The first date carved at the site is AD 435 and is found on Altar 13, in front of Structure 40.[4] Most of the buildings and monuments visible today were the result of the building efforts of two kings who were father and son, Itzamnaaj Balam (Shield Jaguar) II and Yaxun Balam (Bird Jaguar) IV.

Shield Jaguar II took power in AD 681 and had a lengthy reign of 60 years.[5] Under this warrior king, Yaxchilán thrived economically and politically. Shield Jaguar II commissioned and built extensive buildings, hieroglyphic stairways, lintels, and stelae. Three of the most impressive carved lintels ever produced in the Mayan world were constructed under his

rule. For much of Yaxchilán's history there was a power struggle between it and a site downriver to the north now named Piedras Negras. During Shield Jaguar II's reign, Piedras Negras's grip on Yaxchilán was loosened and he declared victory and independence.[6] This shift in power most likely led to an increased amount of wealth for the city, as Yaxchilán exerted more control over river traffic along the Usumacinta.[7] It is still unknown how a site as relatively small as Yaxchilán could have been so successful in battle to wield so much power over other cities in the region. Shield Jaguar II died at the age of 95 in 742, leaving an opening for kingship that lasted for ten years.[8]

In 752, after a ten-year contest to the throne, his son Bird Jaguar IV finally took power.[9] The decade-long delay is still somewhat of a mystery. It may have been due to the fact he was required to produce an heir to the throne before becoming king or possibly because of the lower status of his mother, Lady Ik Skull from the distant superpower Calakmul.[10] She was a second wife that Shield Jaguar II married when he was 61; his first and primary wife was

## BOOK OF MORMON COMPARISONS

*The known parts of Yaxchilán's history occurred centuries after the close of the Book of Mormon. However, it is set in a desirable location that probably attracted settlers centuries before its written record. Especially notable is the Usumacinta River, which is an important landmark and may relate to Book of Mormon geography. Also within the site itself are some very interesting similarities that are worth looking into.*

### Records in Stone

Yaxchilán is a great place to see examples of Mayan carvings and inscriptions on stone lintels, stelae, and walls. Much of what we know about the Maya has been shaped by the written records inscribed on these stone monuments. The idea that stone monuments recorded actual events is relatively new. Before the 1960s, the traditional view was that these monuments only depicted mythical beings and deities. When theories surfaced that the stelae might be records of actual events, some scholars reacted strongly. For example, in 1946 Sylvanus Morley said, "The Maya inscriptions . . . tell no story of kingly conquests, recount no deeds of imperial achievement. . . . It is even probable that the name glyphs of specific men and women were never recorded upon the Maya monuments."[27] To the suggestion that real people and events were carved on stelae, J. Eric S. Thompson, the acknowledged authority on Mayan archaeology for most of the twentieth century, said in 1950, "To me such a possibility is well-nigh inconceivable." Faced with undeniable evidence to the

*(continued on page 57)*

By 4:00 a.m., trucks or buses began driving past our makeshift camp, honking their horns and making all kinds of noise. Needless to say, this was not one of our better nights of sleep, but we did learn the importance of putting on a rain fly in the proper direction and orientation.

We were eventually fully awakened later in the morning by the sounds of horses, chickens, and pigs as we emerged from our tents to find that we had made camp near the middle of town. Pigs and all kinds of domesticated animals greeted us as we packed up our tents and supplies. In the morning light, we could see that Co-op Bethel was a very small, isolated town with few amenities. We walked a block or two farther and entered a small restaurant, considering ourselves lucky to have found a bathroom that we could use for the morning. Asking around for the Posada Maya, we were told that it did not exist anymore and not to consider it as an option for staying at Bethel. At least now we know why we could never get through to it on the phone, no matter how often we tried.

(continued on page 58)

*Not the most luxurious of accommodations, but at midnight, travelers cannot be choosers.*

Lady Xoc from the Yaxchilán nobility.[11] Why his local wife did not provide an heir to the throne is not known, neither is the reason he took a second wife (not a common occurrence) from such a distant site as Calakmul. Some politics must have been involved somewhere. We do not know how Lady Xoc reacted to this, but she has the distinction of being the only known Mayan woman to have a building glorifying her, Structure 23 in the Main Plaza.[12] Perhaps Shield Jaguar II had some politics to take care of at home as well.

Upon taking the throne, Bird Jaguar IV followed Shield Jaguar II's example, commissioning many new buildings at Yaxchilán. But unlike his father, Bird Jaguar IV's building program seemed to be aimed more at legitimizing his own legacy and justifying himself as king. Perhaps his status as the son of a foreign, lesser queen was causing him trouble. He carved over existing texts to create his own hieroglyphic stairway, which gave a dynastic history of Yaxchilán from the foundation of the city to his own kingship. In addition, Bird Jaguar IV destroyed earlier texts, reset historical king lists, and erased and recarved monuments.[13] Bird Jaguar IV's rule ended with his death in 768. His long campaign to solidify his position apparently worked, and his son Shield Jaguar III acceded to the throne in AD 771.[14]

The last recorded date of AD 808 at Yaxchilán is found in Building 3. Some archaeological evidence suggests that the city was attacked and its inhabitants killed in one great final battle which eventually overwhelmed the city.[15] Other sites like Bonampak and Piedras Negras along the Usumacinta suffered violence or sudden abandonment at about the same time, so it is possible that a large-scale war engulfed the entire region. Most likely the site was totally abandoned around AD 900.[16] Yaxchilán then lay silent and deserted for untold centuries, perhaps known only to the Lacandón, a local Mayan tribe distinguished by the long, straight hair and white tunics worn by its men. They seem to have known about the site for a long time and continue to come here to perform religious rituals. Traces of burned copal, a local resin used as incense, can still be seen in sacred areas around the site.

The first confirmed modern visitor to Yaxchilán was the Mexican explorer and army officer Juan Galindo, who stopped here in 1833 while navigating the river. In 1881, Edwin Rockstroh, a professor at a college in Guatemala, wrote a brief report about the site. After reading this description, the English explorer Alfred Maudslay arrived at Yaxchilán in 1882. A mere two days later, Désiré Charnay also found the site and was disappointed to have been beaten by the English amateur. However, Maudslay graciously conceded the credit to the Frenchman, who named the site Ciudad Lorillard.[17] But Maudslay's work at Yaxchilán was to have a greater impact. He photographed, explored, and mapped the city, removing eight of the finest lintels to ship to England; most are still in the British Museum.

The Austrian explorer Teobert Maler first visited Yaxchilán in 1895 and returned many times to discover more buildings and stelae and published many of his findings. He is the one who gave this site the name that it still has today. In 1931, Sylvanus Morley from the Carnegie Institute arrived to study the site, but no excavations were performed. His main accomplishment was to produce the site map that is still in use. Decades then passed without

*(Records in Stone continued)* contrary, he finally admitted he was mistaken two decades later.[28]

It was not until Tatiana Proskouriakoff wrote two articles on Yaxchilán, in addition to one on Piedras Negras, in the early 1960s, that ideas about Mayan stone monuments began to change. She studied the lintels of these two sites and realized that they were not portraits of mythical beings, but portrayals of actual people and historical records. Looking back on her discoveries, she said, "In retrospect, the idea that Maya texts record history, naming the rulers or lords of the towns, seems so natural that it is strange it has not been thoroughly explored before."[29] Stela 12 at Yaxchilán is an example of such royal history, recording a king's death, transfer of power, the results of battle, and rituals. A loose translation of its text reads, "On 19 June AD 742 the ruler, Shield Jaguar II, died. He was an incense offerer and was more than 78 years old. He was guardian of the captive Ah Nik. And then it came to pass that 3,606 days forward, to reach the date 3 May AD 752 when Bird Jaguar IV was seated as lord. He is the guardian of Ah Uk. He is like the sky god. He is the divine lord of Yaxchilán. He is the stood up one."[30]

Omni 20–22 relates that sometime after Mosiah discovered Zarahemla and was appointed king, he was given a large stone with engravings on it that the people of Zarahemla had found. They were not able to read it, but he was able to through the (continued on page 59)

Our first priority (after the bathroom) was to hire a boat to take us to Yaxchilán. Our overly optimistic plan had been to visit it the previous afternoon, leaving this day open for Bonampak and possibly Palenque. We did not know if we could fit it all in, but if we did, it would mean leaving our rental car here while we stayed overnight in Mexico, an option that seemed a little risky to us. But many times, problems like these can be solved with help from the locals. Knowing Spanish in this situation proved to be almost a necessity.

At a small kiosk, one of us who spoke Spanish bought some drinks and snacks and tried to find out how we might make our travel arrangements. There we met Señor Brillones, who ran the store and was very helpful. He told us that his son-in-law Milton could take us on his boat down the river to the site. When we told him our concerns about leaving the car overnight, he said that would be no problem. Pleased at our good fortune, we made plans to leave at 8:00 a.m. and found that his daughter Ludi, Milton's wife, could watch our car for us at their home overnight while we went to Yaxchilán and farther into Mexico. We took some time before leaving to have a breakfast of fried chicken and potatoes outside the kiosk, which was surprisingly good.

After our meal, we drove down another dirt path to Milton and Ludi's house, really just a shack at the edge of the jungle, and dropped our car off with her. Then we walked down to the river where he was waiting for us. Arriving at the muddy riverbank an hour after we said we would, we

(continued on page 60)

any work being done here.[18] Oddly enough, for such an important site, very little excavation work has been done at Yaxchilán; most of what we know about its history comes from the decipherment of texts.

During the early 1960s, Russian-born archaeologist Tatiana Proskouriakoff studied the Mayan hieroglyphs at Yaxchilán and its neighboring rival Piedras Negras. From her studies, she was the first to discover that the dates on stone monuments were in periods roughly equivalent to the length of human life spans, and therefore they were historical texts whose images depicted real people.[19] This suggestion ran counter to the prevailing belief at the time. Her discovery and success in deciphering hieroglyphs revolutionized Mayan archaeology and eventually overturned the commonly-held belief in the scholarly community that the monuments were nothing more than depictions of esoteric Mayan deities and beliefs. Finally in 1972, Roberto García Moll with INAH headed the Proyecto Yaxchilán and began the first excavations. His team cleared and restored over half of the buildings and made some major finds.[20] But there still are unrestored areas closed to tourists and much more work could be done that would answer many questions about Yaxchilán's history.

## BRIEF SITE OVERVIEW

Built in the hills along the western bank of the Usumacinta River, Yaxchilán is one of the most beautiful sites we visited. It is located on the southeast corner of the Chiapas region and can only be accessed by boat or small plane. The abundance of wildlife in the rain forests and river, along with the natural protection provided by the hills near the bank, combined to make this site a natural place to settle. Many impressive stelae, hieroglyphic writing, and some of the most brilliantly carved lintels ever found in the Mayan world come from Yaxchilán. If you have ever fantasized about exploring pristine, ancient ruins in the middle of a remote jungle, this is the right place.

Once you disembark from the boat and pay the entrance fee, you have the option of taking one of two paths into the site. Walking ahead and to the left takes you directly into the main plaza, and the path to the right takes you the back way up a hill to the more secluded West Acropolis. Most visitors will probably take the path toward the main plaza; we turned right and eventually were glad we did. The trail took us up a steep hill, using smooth, slippery rocks as steps, through the jungle to reach the West Acropolis.

As we approached the structures at the top of the hill, we were filled with anticipation for this moment. We had purchased three expensive volumes of the *Corpus of the Maya Hieroglyphic Inscriptions* from the Peabody Museum, which gave great descriptions and drawings of most of the carvings at Yaxchilán. Quite a few of them contained the hieroglyphic phrase "it came to pass," and the West Acropolis would provide us with our first glimpses of this coveted glyph. They were located on the hieroglyphic stairway at Temple 44, which Shield Jaguar II built to celebrate his victories in war.[21] Much to our dismay, the stairway was extremely eroded and just looked like regular stone steps. Fortunately, each of the three doorways above the hieroglyphic steps did hold some very interesting lintels that depict Shield Jaguar taking hold of his captives by the topknots of their heads. The lintels seemed like

*(records in stone continued)* power of God. His translation follows a pattern similar to that found on many stelae in Mesoamerica. The stone gave an account of King Coriantumr, the results of a battle, and a history of his fathers. Usually, Mayan stelae document the same kinds of events.

At the time of the Book of Mormon's publication, the existence of such stone monuments in ancient America was not known. They first came to the public's knowledge a decade later with the publication of Stephens and Catherwood's first volume, but 130 years would pass before it was generally acknowledged that these monuments were indeed historical records.

*Stela 11, showing Bird Jaguar IV performing rituals to establish his right to be king*

boarded his boat and started our journey down the Usumacinta River to Yaxchilán.

This was our third morning in Guatemala, and we were finally on our way to see some ruins, so our excitement level was high. We had agreed on a total price of $100 for Milton to take us down to the site, wait for two hours, then take us back up the river and drop us off at Frontera Corozal in Mexico. According to guidebooks, this is an average fee, and the more people you include in your excursion, the cheaper it will be for each one. The boat, called a lancha, was shaped like a 15-foot narrow canoe with a thatch-covered open canopy in the middle. Milton sat in the back of the boat, driving us down the river with a small outboard motor. The ride down the river lasted about 45 minutes. As we neared the site, we could see ruins peeking through the jungle from the boat. We pulled up to the river's edge and prepared to get out, leaving our packs in the lancha. Knowing that we had a limited time to see the site, we hurried off the boat and up the steep trail that led to the ruins.

*No matter what, do not put the head back on the body, unless it is the year 2012.*

replicas, since they sounded hollow when we tapped them with our hands. We know that some of them have been removed and replaced with replicas. They are well made and in many cases the only way to distinguish the real from the authentic is to tap them to see how they sound and feel.

Archaeological evidence suggests that a major battle took place at the West Acropolis. Over 200 projectile points have been found in the rubble here. They were mainly made of flint and were used on darts, perhaps propelled by *atlatls*, a weapon of central Mexico.[22] This area could have been the setting of the final assault that ended in Yaxchilán's permanent defeat.

From the West Acropolis we headed south, descending and then ascending more hills on smooth rock steps, made even slipperier by the intermittent rain, toward Buildings 39, 40, and 41. These structures are situated on what is known as the Large Acropolis, even though it is smaller than the West Acropolis, sometimes referred to as the Small Acropolis. There is not much to see at these three temples. In front of Temple 40 is Stela 12, which contains some glyphic writing that can barely be discerned, and Stela 13, which portrays some unknown ruler, but is also badly eroded. Temple 40 used to be covered with murals but has unfortunately decayed so there was nothing left to see. We had hoped again to find our much anticipated glyph at Temple 41 but found no glyphic writing whatsoever. For the moment, it appeared that we were not going to find the "it came to pass" glyph after all. Perhaps this was the reason we were not able to find more references to this glyph in LDS literature.

We continued down and then up the trail

toward the back of Temple 33, Yaxchilán's most famous structure, also called the Palace. This building is impressive, sitting on the top of the hill and sporting a tall roofcomb. As we walked around to the front, we went directly to the hieroglyphic stairway located below the three doors that led inside the building. The central step depicts Bird Jaguar IV playing the Mesoamerican ball game with his ancestors; bound captives are used (obviously symbolically) in place of the ball. As we studied the central step, we finally came upon what we wanted to see most: the "it came to pass" glyph. There were three located on the left side of the central step, which depicts Bird Jaguar IV hitting the ball (victim) against the hieroglyphic stairway containing the coveted glyphs. We could not have been happier; the glyphs were in a very good state of preservation and easy to decipher.

## The River Sidon

The location of the River Sidon has been a subject of debate among LDS scholars, and no definitive consensus had been reached. If the Book of Mormon took place in Mesoamerica, the only viable candidates for the River Sidon are the Grijalva and the Usumacinta rivers. They both start in the Guatemalan Highlands, branch away from each other heading roughly to the north and northwest, and empty into the Gulf of Mexico. We leave the debate to authors like John Sorenson, Richard Hauk, and Joseph Allen, who each give good arguments for the rivers and for overall Book of Mormon geography, although they reach differing conclusions. Sorenson favors the Grijalva,[32] Hauk the Usumacinta,[33] and Allen has vacillated between the two as the modern-day River Sidon.[34] What we do know is that Zarahemla was near the river on its west bank and that it was an important landmark for much of Book of Mormon history. Other Book of Mormon sites were also located along its west bank.

Whether or not the Usumacinta was the ancient River Sidon depends mainly on where Zarahemla was located, and that may never be known. We do know that the Usumacinta does have ancient sites along its west bank,[35] and the region was inhabited during Book of

(continued on page 63)

In the relatively well-preserved roofcomb, a seated figure on a throne is thought to be either Bird Jaguar IV or his son. The three doorways open into a hallway with four alcoves or small rooms. The lintels above the doorways contain scenes that solidify Bird Jaguar IV's claim to power, but we were mostly interested in the central one. This lintel shows Shield Jaguar III with his father on his right, both holding the bird cross staff. These cross-shaped staffs symbolize the world tree and the point where heaven and earth meet and are associated with sacrificial blood by a current and future king; on the top is the celestial bird deity.[23] In one room of this temple sits a statue of Bird Jaguar IV, but his head is in another room. If you are lucky enough to be there on the summer solstice, the sun will shine directly on the statue. The Lacandón Maya believe that if the head is put back on the statue's body, this cycle of the world will end.[24] We are not sure how this belief started, but they have used these rooms for religious ceremonies and burning incense.

Walking down from Temple 33 offered an incredible view of the main plaza. The hill is high and a bit steep, but the climb down is well worth it. Large ceiba trees and rainforest line the path and surround the plaza below. The impressive view of the area coming down the hill is much of the reason we think the route around the back of the city we took was the right choice. Seeing the plaza for the first time from this vantage point added greatly to the beauty of the site. We walked to the bottom of the grassy plaza straight to Stela 1, the largest monument at the site. From here we began exploring the plaza. There are many smaller buildings that border the grassy plaza floor. It gives the impression that the plaza was an important community and cultural area, but the buildings themselves are not particularly impressive in their current state. What amazed us was the amount of hieroglyphs we found throughout these smaller buildings. As we explored and attempted to read the writing, we were most astonished at just how many "it came to pass" glyphs were found throughout the buildings there. The only conclusion we could draw from this was that the use of this term in Mayan writing was very common, not very different from what we read in the Book of Mormon.

Buildings 22, 23, and 24 all have the "it came to pass" glyph. Temple 23 is the most famous of the three and is dedicated to Lady Xoc, Shield Jaguar II's first wife. This building housed Lintels 24, 25, and 26, arguably the finest carved structures anywhere in the Mayan world. Unfortunately, the original Lintels 24 and 25 are at the British Museum in London, with 26 housed in the national museum in Mexico City. The famous hieroglyphic stairway is found near the northwest corner of the plaza. The stairway contains the longest text at the site and details the history of Yaxchilán's kings from the founder to Bird Jaguar IV,[25] who may have recarved some to suit his purposes. The six steps are very worn and at first glance appear to be unadorned. Included in the text are several more examples of the "it came to pass" glyph, but the steps are so eroded and moss-covered that nothing can be made out today. From the top of the stairway, a mound of stones in the river can be seen, which may have served as the base of a bridge to the other side. Nearby in the northwestern corner, Stela 11 lies on the ground under a protective roof. Originally from the West Acropolis, this monument depicts Bird Jaguar and his father in a kingly ritual meant to show the transfer of kingship. In 1966, an attempt was made to move this stela from the site to Mexico City. It was brought by riverboat to Agua Azul and readied for shipment by plane. The stela was found to be too heavy for air transport and was later returned to the site.[26]

With our limited time we were unable to fully explore the entire plaza, but the two hours we had were just about enough to get a good feel for the site. An hour or two more would be nice if you would like to see all there is to see at a more leisurely pace. There is a lot to see in the plaza, some of which is located to the southwest and not currently open to the public, perhaps because it has not been completely explored or excavated. Even with our short time there, we feel very fortunate to have visited Yaxchilán. In 1988, a dam was planned for the Usumacinta River, which would have raised the water level and flooded many sites along its banks, including this one. Data from satellite imaging was shown to the Guatemalan and Mexican presidents, who intervened and stopped the project.[27] We just cannot imagine the great loss to the historical record if this dam had been built.

*(River Sidon continued)* Mormon times. It is interesting that according to Mosiah 8:8, in trying to find Zarahemla, Limhi's group got lost and ended up finding the remnants of the Jaredite civilization. If they had been trying to follow the modern-day Usumacinta back and mistakenly followed the Grijalva, this could explain what happened. Since both rivers start near each other in the Guatemalan Highlands, this would be an easy error to make.

## "And It Came to Pass"

Various LDS scholars have commented on a Mayan glyph that can be translated as "it came to pass." Our first introduction to this concept was through the work of Joseph Allen, who only mentions this glyph as found in the Temple of the Inscriptions at Palenque. Through our own research, we discovered that additional examples of this glyphic phrase can be found at other sites, including at Piedras Negras on Stela 3. This site downriver from Yaxchilán is in an even more remote section of Guatemalan jungle and few tourists visit it.

Notwithstanding the additional time and cost, we considered going to see it ourselves until we learned that the stela had been cut up and taken by looters. Disappointed, we continued our search for other examples, eventually finding many at Yaxchilán.

Understandably, we were excited at the prospect of finally seeing this glyph for ourselves. From our study of archaeological folios, we found at least 23 instances of this phrase just at Yaxchilán. Unfortunately, many of them have been so eroded by centuries of neglect in this jungle setting that they are now illegible. However, we found four very good examples in Hieroglyphic Steps VII and VIII to Building 33, Bird Jaguar IV's crowning achievement in aggrandizing himself. The steps are protected by a modern overhang that looks sturdy and permanent, so they should last for future visitors to appreciate.

|  |  |  |  |  |
|---|---|---|---|---|
| i-u-t(i) (iwal-ut) | u-ti (ut) | i | u | ti |
| *and then it occurred* *and then it came to pass* | *to occur* *to come to pass* | *and then* *posterior date indicator* | *he, she, it* *his, hers, its* | *phonetic sign* *on, to, from, with, at* |

|  |  |  |  |
|---|---|---|---|
| u-ti-ya (utiy) | u | ti | ya |
| *since it came to pass* *anterior date indicator* | *he, she, it* *his, hers, its* | *phonetic sign* *on, to, from, with, at* | *phonetic sign* *completive aspect* |

*adapted from John Montgomery, Dictionary of Maya Hieroglyphs*

Studying a bit more about Mayan hieroglyphs, we discovered that they form an extremely complex and not fully understood writing system. The same word can be written in many ways by using figurative pictures, phonetic signs, or a combination of the two. The phrase for "it came to pass" contains three phonetic elements that combine to make the complete phrase. Joseph Allen broke this glyph apart and described the sound of each separate sign, but based on Mayan dictionaries we have studied, we believe that he has made some errors. This phrase can be written many ways with different combinations, but there are basically two versions: *i-u-ti* (pronounced i-ut or iwal-ut), which can be translated as "and then it came to pass," and *utiya* (pronounced utiy), which can be translated as "it had come to pass." In spoken Mayan, the last vowel after the consonant is often dropped.

We soon realized that this is an extremely common phrase in ancient Mayan writings and is usually connected to the passage of time. It is so pervasive that it seems like any site that has carved texts will have *i-u-ti* or *utiya* among them, as we will see with other sites that we visited. Although this phrase also appears in the King James Version of the Bible, it has been an excuse for criticism and ridicule from opponents of the Book of Mormon, especially for its frequency. Now we see that this phrase is actually a strong support for the authenticity of this ancient American scripture, for not only was it used anciently, but it was frequently used by literate people in the very region where the Book of Mormon is supposed to have taken place.

## Mayan Cross

Cross-shaped staffs, or the bird cross staff as they are sometimes called, are important religious symbols to the Maya. They represent the world tree, where the earth and heavens meet. This tree was an important feature of their religion, representing creation, resurrection, and a pathway to the heavens and deification.[36] For more detailed information on the world tree, see the chapter on Palenque. At the top of each staff is a bird that

*Lintel 2 of Building 33*

symbolizes Itzamná, a Mayan god that has many similarities to Jesus Christ.[37] The bird cross staffs on the lintels of Building 33 appear to be associated with sacrifice, particularly that of the spilling of blood by a present and future king. Archaeologists today would deny that the Maya made any association with Christ in this symbol, yet the parallels lead us to wonder if it is not really a huge stretch to at least present it as a possibility. Mayan kings were anxious to associate themselves with this symbol as a sign of their divine right to reign. Perhaps its true meaning, like many religious doctrines, had changed over hundreds of years by the time Building 33 was built.

# Final Battles

There is archaeological evidence that war was one of the factors that caused the decline of Mayan cities along the Usumacinta. The West Acropolis is built on an elevated hill, making it easily defendable and an ideal vantage point for a battle. When this area was explored, it was found to be covered with 217 projectile points, signifying that a great battle had occurred there. Some archaeologists believe that a great battle marked the end of the city's history, imagining a surviving group of Yaxchilán's leaders and common citizens retreating from a battle in the outskirts of the city. They would have taken refuge on the hill of the West Acropolis to defend themselves against a final assault of their enemies.

The Book of Mormon describes a similar battle, although on a larger scale. For the battle that resulted in the end of the Nephite nation, Mormon records in Mormon 6:2–4 that the armies gathered around a hill named Cumorah. After the great slaughter, the few survivors, including Mormon and Moroni, retreated to the top of the hill to escape their enemies and survey their surroundings. It is possible that a similar event took place on this hill at Yaxchilán.

# Temple Dedications

Every Mesoamerican site has temples of various kinds. Usually their names were given to them by Spanish conquerors or modern-day explorers and archaeologists. We doubt the ancient Maya would have recognized these contemporary labels, and perhaps much of these buildings' original purpose and significance has been lost. It is even possible that some of the structures we call temples today were not thought of as such by their original builders.

What makes a temple different from another building? Recent translations of hieroglyphic texts demonstrate that the Maya performed temple dedication ceremonies, which were important enough to be written down. Many of these texts have been found at Yaxchilán, recorded in stone.[38] Most likely, buildings were not considered sacred until after the dedication was completed. Temples at Yaxchilán have their openings facing toward the east and the rising sun, a symbol of heat and goodness to the ancient Maya.[39] Although now densely covered in trees and jungle undergrowth, these terraces and hills used to be free of any vegetation, allowing a clear view of the movement of the rising sun each morning.

# MEXICO: CROSSING THE USUMACINTA RIVER

There are several different routes to Mexico from Guatemala. The most popular involves crossing the Usumacinta River into the state of Chiapas at Frontera Corozal from either Bethel or the nearby village of La Técnica. Another option is driving west from Flores to El Naranjo, and then across the San Pedro River to La Palma in Mexico. The most difficult option may be traveling by river from Sayaxché to Benemérito, Mexico and then up the Usumacinta. Although the last two routes mentioned are possible, they do require more time and additional planning, as there are no regular boat schedules on either of the routes. We crossed the border from Bethel on the Usumacinta and found it to be a great way to go.

Before leaving Guatemala, you must visit the border control station several minutes south of Bethel, located in a small building on the left side of the road on the way out of town. Here we showed our passports and paid a small fee in exchange for a stamp granting permission to depart Guatemala and enter Mexico. Supposedly this transaction is communicated to border control in Mexico, so if you decide not to pay the fee and get the stamp and are caught, you could end up in a serious situation or owe a large fine. Some guidebooks may mention that it is not necessary to pay a fee to get your passport stamped, but if you take this high ground, you may only be rewarded with extra delays and hassle. The interesting part of all this is there is no one waiting at the river to make sure you can officially cross the border. If you do not know about the need for this little process, it is very easy to end up in Mexico illegally. After all, it is only a river in a very remote area, and none of the locals ask for documentation when they take you across. Upon returning to Guatemala after visiting Mexico, it is necessary to stop at the same office when leaving Bethel for a Guatemalan entry stamp, but there is no fee for this procedure.

While waiting for approval, we exchanged quetzals for pesos with people working at the office. This made it easy so we did not have to look for a place to exchange money when we got to Mexico. We also had someone approach us and suggest taking our car into Mexico by boat. When we questioned how this worked, he carefully explained the process: a wooden

*One of the river's locals checking us out*

platform would be laid across two *lanchas*, or long, thin canoes. After driving onto the platform, the boats would ferry the vehicle across the river and into Mexico. This was casually described as a simple process, but we could not tell if they were joking. Although it initially sounded like a great idea, we decided against it and felt justified when we saw the little canoe-like *lanchas* and the size or the river. We cannot in any way imagine that this would have been a good idea, even if the offer was serious. In any case, we do not recommend it. The image of a rental car sliding off this precarious platform and sinking to the bottom of the river in the middle of nowhere is not a pleasant one.

Rather than travel to Corozal, we headed farther downstream, directly to the incredible site of Yaxchilán. This took around 45 minutes, boating along with the current. We had previously arranged for our boatman to wait for us at the edge of the ruins and to take us directly to Corozal, instead of returning us to Bethel. Guidebooks suggest that a price of about US $100 is what this kind of travel arrangement will cost, and we found that to be correct.

Because of the steady current, the ride back upstream took almost twice as long. But we enjoyed it; the time spent on the river was amazing. The remote and exotic setting really added to the excitement of the adventure. The small boat sat just inches above the water and moved quickly though the river, powered by a small outboard motor. The Usumacinta slowly meanders though the dense Petén jungle, giving you the feeling of being somewhere ancient and otherworldly. Besides the occasional person spotted on the banks of the river or the small number of boats we passed, we felt alone, as if we were exploring uncharted territories. On our way back upstream we saw several large crocodiles on the banks of the river. Milton, our boatman, took us in for a closer look. As we approached an amazingly still crocodile, it suddenly sprang to life and lunged into the water as if it was going to wreak havoc on our little vessel. Luckily, we saw no further sign of it as it was just probably trying to get away from us. However, this did answer the question we had earlier when we were considering how safe it was to swim in the river.

After Yaxchilán, Milton dropped us off at the border town of Frontera Corozal. Some maps and books have it listed as Frontera Echeverría, but we did not hear anyone here call it that. Frontera just means "frontier" in Spanish, so the locals simply refer to the town as Corozal.

# BONAMPAK

procession of musicians

ancient defacements

Chan Muan on Stela 1

69

## How We Got There

Bonampak was not far away from Corozal, and since it was still early in the day, we discussed the possibility of seeing Palenque as well. It seemed a shame to have crossed into Mexico and be so close to such an important site, yet not see it. Unanimously we decided to go for it. This meant that after having visited Yaxchilán that morning, we would see Bonampak this afternoon and spend the night at Palenque. The next day we would tour Palenque, return to the border, cross the river, and drive to Tikal to spend the night there. This was certainly a tight schedule, but we had planned a great deal of flexibility into this trip and we were confident we could do it. We doubt that many visitors to these sites would do the same as we did, but it can be done.

Our impromptu route would require precision planning and a fast means of traveling without delays. The first step was to make arrangements. We had looked up a bus schedule before leaving the States to assist in this leg of our trip, and we were now at the bus stop by the river. After asking around for information on how to get to Bonampak and Palenque, we settled on a taxi that took us to a sort of bus depot a few blocks into town. There we made arrangements for a bus

(continued on page 72)

70

## BACKGROUND

Anciently, Bonampak was known as Aké,[1] but not much has been published about the origins of the site. The earliest ceramics excavated here may date as far back as AD 100,[2] but no buildings from the first few centuries of its settlement remain. Its first significant king was named Bird Jaguar (a common royal name in these parts), and he reigned sometime in the first half of the fifth century, AD.[3] Most of what survives today at Bonampak dates to the latter half of the Classic period, and we know the most about its last king, Chan Muan, who ascended to the throne in AD 776.[4] From what we can tell, Bonampak was never a major power in the region and always seems to have been dominated by either Yaxchilán or Piedras Negras,[5] perhaps dependent on which one was in control at the time.

Whether by force or by political astuteness, Chan Muan married a noblewoman from Yaxchilán, perhaps the sister of Shield Jaguar II, the reigning king at that city.[6] The murals for which Bonampak is famous were painted

during Chan Muan's reign and depict a battle and its aftermath. According to texts accompanying the murals, he began this battle at the command of Lacanhá, a neighboring site.[7] Other sources suggest that he accompanied Yaxchilán's king into battle, so we are not sure which version is correct, but the ties to Yaxchilán are undeniable. The story told by the murals was thought to commence in Room 1, where a royal child is presented. The child is related to Shield Jaguar II,[8] but whether it is his or Chan Muan's son is not known. At any rate, the child seems destined for kingship at Bonampak, and the battle is undertaken to obtain sacrificial victims for the occasion. According to some glyphs, Shield Jaguar may have participated in the fighting.[9] The last set of murals depicts a victory celebration and another Yaxchilán king, Itzamnaaj Balam III, presiding over the accession of the new Bonampak king in 790.[10]

This period of prosperity seems not to have lasted long, however, as the last date recorded at Bonampak is AD 792.[11] For some unrecorded reason, the famous murals were

## BOOK OF MORMON COMPARISONS

*Bonampak's origins may reach back into the last centuries of Book of Mormon history, and it is likely that its location fits into the geographical limits of the scriptural record. However, most of its early history has been all but obliterated and the events depicted on its murals took place centuries after the Nephite nation was destroyed. Still, the unprecedented discovery of its murals provided insight into previously unknown details of Mesoamerican history that have been overlooked or ignored for much of the twentieth century.*

### Warfare

Once they came to light, the violent scenes of battle and the aftermath of human sacrifice gave archaeologists a greater understanding of the interest among Mayan rulers in waging war.[24] The murals' discovery is important because the events depicted were in conflict with the prevailing beliefs about the Classic period that were held for much of the twentieth century. In his 1955 report on the murals, the pre-eminent Mayan scholar J. Eric S. Thompson concentrated on the dancers and musicians in Room 1, downplaying the imagery of war and sacrifice, ostensibly because they conflicted with his belief that the Mayan Classic period was a peaceful time of progress when they reached the heights of their civilization.[25] It is lamentable that the recognized authority on Mayan culture would ignore evidence in order to maintain the status quo, but eventually enough discoveries were made so that the prevailing opinion evolved to fit the findings. However, this is not the only such instance of discarding facts.

(continued on page 73)

passing by the turnoff to Bonampak later in the afternoon to pick us up and take us to Palenque. We haggled a bit and all settled on an overall price for all the buses and taxis involved in getting us from here to there. Split three ways, it was not overly expensive.

The taxi driver took us out of Corozal, which was larger than we had previously imagined, heading on the road to the Bonampak turnoff, some 25 kilometers away. Thankfully, he understood our need for haste and sped along the curvy yet well-paved road through the jungle at a breakneck pace. We just held on and hoped he knew what he was doing. Before too long, we arrived at the crossroads of San Javier and Bonampak, where a road to the left led to the site. For some reason we did not fully understand, standard buses and taxis are not allowed to take tourists down this road, so we were dropped off and our taxi returned to town.

From there we took a local taxi to the ruins. Our driver was Margarito, a Mayan guide who took visitors to the site; his wife ran a restaurant at the crossroads. As he drove us along the road to Bonampak in his taxi (which looked just like the taxi that brought us here), he told us his Mayan name, which we do not remember, but he did say that it meant "Little Bird." The bumpy ride along the rough road did not take long, and as he let us out at the entrance, we agreed on a time to return to the main road, allowing enough time to eat lunch at his restaurant before catching the bus to Palenque.

never finished.[12] An outbreak of fighting, perhaps in retaliation for the battle depicted in Bonampak's murals, likely consumed the area about this time and brought swift destruction to cities along the Usumacinta River. Archaeological evidence suggests that Piedras Negras was burned and even the great Yaxchilán may have been the scene of a last, desperate defense against a final assault that brought a quick end to its dominion in the area.[13] It is likely that Bonampak suffered a similar fate around this time.

The site was abandoned as the peak of the Mayan civilization moved northward into the Yucatán. For centuries it remained empty and desolate, overtaken by the jungle and unknown to outsiders. The Lacandón, a local Mayan tribe whose men traditionally grow their hair long and straight and wear white robes, may have known about the site and had particular superstitions about it. They live in such deep, remote jungle that they largely avoided contact with outsiders until the twentieth century. Perhaps from their legends, the Austrian explorer Teobert Maler heard about ruins in this area in 1898.[14] Margarito told us that an ancestor of his found the site while hunting deer in the nearby jungle. We are not sure how much credence to give his story, or if he was referring to someone who found it initially or who led foreign explorers to it.

The actual discovery of Bonampak in the 1940s reads like some kind of lurid Hollywood drama. In 1943, Danish archaeologist Frans Blom hired Karl Frey, an American draft dodger, to guide him in an expedition through this area. He came very close to Bonampak but succumbed to malaria and had to be carried back. Frey and a veteran named John Bourne (heir to the Singer Sewing Machine fortune) actually found the site in 1946 with the help of two Lacandón guides.[15] They saw the plaza with its stelae and structures, but that is about all. The Lacandón did not know about the murals, having never entered the buildings, perhaps out of superstition. Later that year, filmmaker Giles Healey arrived at Bonampak with the same Lacandón guides. He is the first one to enter the buildings and see the murals. His photographs created a worldwide stir and began what would later be called "Bonampakitis."[16] The disaffected Karl Frey, who by now had renounced his American citizenship and was calling himself "Carlos," claimed that he was the actual discoverer of Bonampak and the controversy began. His suspicious death a few years later while heading another expedition to Bonampak would only add to the mystery.

In 1947, a Carnegie Institute team led by Karl Ruppert and none other than J. Eric S. Thompson mapped the site and copied the murals. But the murals were deteriorating and accusations began flying. From 1960 to 1962, Raúl Pavón Abreu with INAH, the Mexican archaeological foundation, cleared the site, restored buildings, built an airstrip, and put a roof over the temple of the murals to protect them.[17] But now that they were kept dry, an opaque crust of salts and minerals began to form over them. It has been suggested that this covering actually protected the paintings and kept them from peeling off the walls, a fate that has befallen other Mayan murals.[18]

INAH continued excavations in 1977 with the main focus of preserving the murals. In the mid-1980s, a team cleaned the walls, removing the salt crust and filling in ancient holes and defacements. By this time, most studies of the

*(Warfare continued)* Often, discoveries that do not fit neatly into the accepted pattern are downplayed or ignored because they cannot be easily explained.

From 2 Nephi to Moroni, the Book of Mormon is replete with accounts of skirmishes, battles, and open war. Around AD 400, Moroni wrote in Mormon 8:8 that not only had the Lamanites destroyed the Nephites, but that they were fighting each other and the entire land was a scene of continual bloodshed, so fierce that he did not know when it would end. As has been shown, these accounts contradicted scholarly opinion until just a few decades ago, regardless of the archaeological work that had been done. This should be a reminder to us that we do not need acceptance in the scholarly community, since they have been wrong before. Now, the Book of Mormon's desperate and nation-ending battles sound much more plausible when viewed against Bonampak's murals and other evidences of destruction along the Usumacinta River. Although the fighting in this area took place long after the last Nephite battle, it is another indication that warfare has been a continual facet of Mesoamerican history.

paintings had only been of the original photographs taken by Healey or early painted copies. Now that the walls were cleaned, a decision was made to fully photograph and document all of the murals. In 1996, the Bonampak Documentation Project, a joint Mexican/American team led by Mary Miller, set about to photograph the paintings with color and infrared film, which would show more clearly the original charcoal lines underneath the paint. Noted archaeologists Stephen Houston (formerly of BYU) and Karl Taube were also involved. FARMS, the Foundation for Ancient Research and Mormon Studies, partially funded the project. Gene Ware and Kirk Duffin of BYU assisted in the digital capture and preparation of images,[19] resulting in what is arguably the most detailed and accurate representation of the murals to date.

## BRIEF SITE OVERVIEW

From the edge of the gravel road, we walked to a small booth, where we paid the entrance fee. A few locals were hanging around the building and we were hoping to see some Lacandón in their traditional garb, but no such luck. They might have been Lacandón, and indeed, Margarito must be if his story is true, but they were all dressed just like everyone else.

From there, we followed a path through the trees into the site. It is surprisingly small, with most of the structures and monuments centered around a modest-sized plaza. Maps show some small buildings away from the main plaza, such as the Frey Group and the Burned Group, but there really is not much else to see. Because of its rather recent discovery and turbulent modern history, we wonder if there is more to be found and excavated in the surrounding jungle. The path crosses a small airstrip that is overgrown with grass. A small plane sits parked (or abandoned) here, right

on the edge of the jungle. Neither the plane nor the airstrip looks like it has been used in some time, although guidebooks may mention that you can fly into Bonampak. We do not know if that is possible now, but judging by appearances, it does not happen very often these days, if at all.

The path took us directly to the plaza, now overgrown with grass and hemmed in by thick jungle all around. To our immediate left was Building 15, a low platform that was fully excavated in 1994. A door has been installed on the top and if you can open it and squeeze inside, you can see a headless, painted sculpture referred to as The Queen. Our attention was fixed solely on the other side of the plaza, so we hurried across, pausing to admire the stelae in the middle. One of them, Stela 1, is cracked and a top portion is missing, but the details are still quite clear. This massive monument originally stood over 12 feet high and portrays Chan Muan, the last king of Bonampak. His image is quite fierce, but knowing the site's subordinate status to other cities in the region, we imagine that his depiction is merely propaganda. Other stelae stand in this area, but none quite as impressive as Chan Muan's portrait.

The Acropolis on the far end of the plaza houses many temples and buildings, but we headed straight for Temple 1, or the Temple of the Paintings. The nondescript outer façade belies the amazing artwork within. Unlike other temples in the Usumacinta region, it does not have a roofcomb, but it does have the standard three doorways and decorated frieze, not much of which has survived. Five niches with ruined figures are spread out above the doorways; the central one contains a statue of Itzamnaaj Balam III, king of Yaxchilán,[20] another indication of the influence exerted over Bonampak in the late Classic period.

The three doorways lead to three separate and unconnected rooms. The beautifully carved stone lintels above the doorways show Chan Muan, Shield Jaguar II, and another king capturing and killing enemies. We filmed and photographed as best we could, but the rooms are dark and there was someone nearby making sure we obeyed the rules, like not using a flash inside and leaving our backpacks outside. The murals inside are apparently meant to be viewed in a sequence, starting not with Room 1 on the left, but with the central Room 2, which was painted before the other two.[21] With this unexpected order, the traditional interpretation described in the background section might be called into question. The information we compiled on Bonampak's history and the interpretation of its murals is somewhat contradictory, so we are not sure what the actual story is.

If the battle depicted in Room 2 took place first, then Rooms 1 and 3 show the fruits of victory in the form of tribute items and allegiance by subjected rulers. The fighting is

## Ethnic Diversity

Immediately apparent upon observing the scenes of battle is that the fight seems to be between two groups of different skin color. They are both darker than what would be considered white, but the difference is unmistakable. According to the murals, the darker group seems to be on the losing end of the fight. It should be mentioned that we have found no scholarly discussion or explanation of this apparent ethnic diversity and why these Maya pictured themselves as a different color than their enemies. In fact, in many copies and digitally-enhanced restorations of the murals, the skin color is adjusted so that there is little to no variation in skin color and all the figures look the same.[26] We find this lack of accuracy in reproducing the murals perplexing and can find no justification for it.

It has been suggested that black figures represent war,[27] or that merchants painted themselves black to represent the dangers of

shown as violent and intense, the aftermath of tortured and sacrificed victims no less graphic. In Room 1, the royal child is shown presented to white-robed nobles, a rarity in Mayan art. Musicians and costumed dancers or actors are also shown. Room 3 shows noble women dressed in white, engaging in ritual bloodletting. A seated woman holds a child, perhaps the same one from Room 1. A sacrificial victim can be seen, carried in. The temple was dedicated in AD 791, but some of the glyphs were left unfinished.[22] It is also interesting to note that some of the faces have intentionally been chipped away and some eyes gouged out of the murals, even on the royal child in Room 1. This could be an example of ritual death applied to those who were in power at Bonampak.

Was a sudden crisis like the outbreak of war responsible, or are there other, less drastic reasons? We may never know for sure, but our knowledge of Bonampak's history, like the extent of the site itself, remains fragmentary. Unexplored structures lie surrounded by thick jungle to the west of the Acropolis and the Lacandón tell stories of additional ruins buried deep in the jungle.[23] It is obvious that what is currently known about Bonampak is only a fragment of what this site has to tell, but the rest of the story may never be known.

traveling as analogous to traveling through the underworld, whose gods are often represented as black.[28] However, that does not seem to be the case with these murals. The simple and obvious answer is that they represent a battle between two different groups of people with differing colors of skin. While this is a later event, it certainly reminds us of the battles between the Nephite and Lamanites, who according to 2 Nephi

5:21, were given a darker skin to distinguish them from the Nephites. It is very possible that even at the end of the eighth century AD, noticeable diversity in skin color still existed.

Perhaps a few thoughts should be shared here about the Lamanite curse. It may be assumed by some that this refers to their dark skin. These doctrines have served as a basis for allegations of racism made against Latter-day Saints. But a careful reading of the scriptures suggests that the difference in skin color was merely a sign to the covenant people. The real curse is a distance from the priesthood of God, and therefore, eternal covenants. Second Nephi 5:20–24 specifically says that because of the curse, the Lamanites hardened their hearts against God and became an idle people. A change in skin color would not do that. The Book of Mormon as well as other scriptures makes it perfectly clear that God is no respecter of persons. People are cursed or removed from blessings by what they do, not who they are.

Included is the warning that the curse would follow the children of those who mixed with the Lamanites. It is easy to see how this can refer to their appearance, but the principal danger is that the children would reject the covenants of God and embrace the foreign culture. By contrast, the Nephites kept themselves apart from the Lamanites and became a peculiar people, similar to the Israelites in the land of Canaan. Just as they considered anyone not of the house of Israel to be a Gentile, the Nephites could have considered anyone besides themselves a Lamanite. Their commandment (for the time being anyway) was to keep to themselves and not mingle with those who would not keep the Lord's commandments. The children of such unions would fall away from the gospel and follow false traditions. They would also inherit the physical appearance or darker skin of the non-Nephite parent. For similar reasons, Church members today are counseled to marry other worthy Church members. This same counsel was given to the Nephites as well as the original Israelites.

In defense of the Lamanites, it must be remembered that father Lehi knew this would happen and spent all of his time exhorting them to change their ways. He also left blessings upon them that someday they would return. The fulfillment of this promise can be seen as the record progresses. The sons of Mosiah became the first missionaries to the Lamanites and were met with much success. It is recorded that the Lamanites who embraced the gospel never fell away again. The first converts even gave their lives for their newfound belief. The same cannot be said of the Nephites. They were constantly falling away, lured into complacency by riches and prosperity. When missionaries tried to preach repentance to these apostates, their success was much more limited.

## Royal Courts and Tribute

Bonampak's murals offer an unparalleled glimpse into the royal courts of ancient Mayan kings. They show a multi-leveled society with servants, performers, warriors, nobles, and the king at the head of it all. Actually, there were several levels of kings in the Mayan hierarchy. The highest king in a sphere of influence was the *kuhul ahaw*, or "divine lord." Subordinate kings were called *y-ahaw* and were often put in power by the higher kings.[29] Chan Muan certainly seems to have been under the kings of Yaxchilán. The white-robed figures probably represent *sahalob*, secondary nobles that ruled under their immediate king.[30] Some higher-level kings rose to that position by defeating other kings in battle, who were then allowed to keep their place if they gave allegiance and tribute to the victorious king.[31] Room 3 appears to show a tribute offering, perhaps as a result of the battle depicted in Room 2. There was no far-reaching Mayan empire like the later Aztecs had. Instead, various Mayan kings ruled over areas that were limited by their own resources and success in battle. Many ruled by the grace and good will of more powerful kings above them.

Kings are mentioned throughout the Book of Mormon. It is significant to point out that kings are not known as being a part of the background of North American natives, the only ancient American culture Joseph Smith or his associates could have had any familiarity with. Many kings existed in fairly close proximity to each other at the same time. Thus, not only was Lamoni a Lamanite king, but his father was a greater king above him, as described in Alma 20:8. The Nephites who returned to the land of Lehi-Nephi were allowed to live there by the Lamanite king, but they were eventually conquered and subjugated. Mosiah 19:15 relates how the defeated king Limhi, son of king Noah, was allowed to remain in power if he delivered a yearly tribute of half of their possessions to the Lamanite king, perhaps in a manner similar to that depicted on the walls at Bonampak.

# PALENQUE

figure in Palace courtyard

Temple of the Foliated Cross

stucco mask of Pakal

## How We Got There

Palenque is such a famous and popular site that you can get to it from practically anywhere in Mexico. Since this leg of our trip began in Guatemala, we were heading there from the opposite direction. Our pre-arranged travel started at the crossroads to Bonampak. Margarito brought us back to his place, where he ran a little restaurant with his wife. We ate a hurried lunch there while our transport waited outside. It turned out to be a little van, crammed with people. We hoped that the delay was not angering them too much; we were cramming our faces as quickly as we could.

Our packs were stowed on a rack on top of the van, and we squeezed in to the last available spaces inside, which was filled with as many people as would fit. There must have been at least ten passengers, using every available bit of seating space and then some. This last trek of our trip from the crossroads of San Javier and Bonampak to the town of Palenque took about two hours, covering a distance of about 146 kilometers. The driver let passengers off at little towns along

*(continued on page 82)*

80

## BACKGROUND

Like most Classic Mayan sites, Palenque's origins date back to the Preclassic period and are shrouded in mystery. Many of the Classic-era buildings cover much earlier structures. Knowledge of its early history is extremely poor, and most of our understanding of its dynasty and relations with other sites comes from records produced in the seventh century AD.[1] The founder of Palenque's dynasty was Kuk Balam I, whose rule began in AD 431 and lasted only four years. One of his titles was Toktan Lord, Toktan referring to an unknown location that was perhaps the home or capital of the original dynasty. This name is used in Palenque's earliest periods. Another name associated with the area was Baak or Baakal, which means "bone" and is the name by which the entire kingdom was known. The actual name of the city of Palenque was Lakamhá, meaning "Great Water" in Mayan.[2] At least six rivers run through the site, an unusual feature in Mayan cities, and are probably the source of this

name. Until name glyphs could finally be deciphered in the twentieth century, no one, not even the local Maya, knew what the site had been called anciently. Since it was so close to the Spanish town of Palenque (named for its defensive palisade), this was the name naturally given to it.

Palenque has a detailed line of dynastic rulers. Its history is unusual in that from AD 583 to AD 604, it was ruled by a queen, Lady Yohl Iknal. She was the only surviving child of the previous king and carried full authority during her reign. A few years after her death, the dynasty was to lose its way again, eventually resulting in a three-year period ruled by a female regent, Lady Sak Kuk. She passed the mantle of rulership to her son, Kinich Hanaab Pakal I, when he was only 12 years old.

Pakal (as he is commonly known today) reigned for almost 70 years and brought Palenque to a new height of power and influence. Much of the large-scale construction took place during his lifetime or that of his son, who commissioned temples and sculptures to honor his successful father and cement his own claim to the throne. Pakal has the honor of being the only Mayan

## BOOK OF MORMON COMPARISONS

*Since Palenque reached its height in the Mayan Classic period, most of the construction visible today is from centuries after the close of the Book of Mormon. However, the location fits and like many sites, the most recent structures were built on top of much earlier ones. There are definitely some important features to look for.*

### Bearded King

Disappointingly, this one is no longer here. A cup carved out of travertine, a soft stone found in caves, is now in the Mesoamerican collection of the Dumbarton Oaks Museum in Washington, D.C. It belonged to the second dynastic king of Palenque, who reigned from AD 435 to 487. The cup contains a carved portrait of this ruler, as well as text identifying it as his. The king is shown as an elderly man with a heavy beard and decidedly non-Mayan features. His name is unknown to historians because, of the two glyphs that make up his name, only the first, *Cha*, has been deciphered. Because the second one resembles a cartoon ghost, he has been given the nickname Casper.[10] Bearded humans and deities are found periodically in Mesoamerican art, but this is notable since the native population is not known for having much facial hair. As far as we know, archaeologists have not given an explanation for this disparity.

*Detail of vase K4332, © Justin Kerr*

81

the way, but the road was direct and we made pretty good time. As we neared our destination, the rain began to fall, increasing in intensity with every passing kilometer. By the time we arrived, it was really coming down.

Entering Palenque from Highway 199, you reach a roundabout with a large sculpture of Pakal's head in the center. To the right is the modern town of Palenque. To the left down the road a few kilometers is the ancient site. We had originally planned to camp out near the ruins, but with such inclement weather, we decided to find a hotel instead. Asking our driver and his young companion where to stay, we were eventually taken to the Mayabell Campground on the road heading to the ruins. Running in through the downpour, we inquired about a room. They had one available for $50, but they would not take credit cards. At that time, we did not have enough cash on hand for such a bill, and deciding that having local currency would be useful anyway, we got our driver to take us back into town to an ATM. We found one along the main drag quite easily and made some withdrawals. Then he took us back to the hotel.

Wanting to reward him for his help and extra efforts, we offered him a bit more than the previously agreed upon price. To our surprise and disappointment, he demanded even more than that, for his extra time and carting us back and forth to the city. We gave in begrudgingly and then tried to arrange transport back to Corozal

(continued on page 84)

king whose name many laypersons have heard, due mainly to the dramatic and unprecedented discovery of his tomb in 1952.

Like most other major Mayan centers, Palenque had both allies and enemies. In the latter category were sites as near as Bonampak and as far away as Calakmul in the southern Yucatán. As an example of the extensive nature of Mayan trade routes and alliances, relations were friendly with Calakmul's continual enemy Tikal, located in the Petén region of northern Guatemala. In fact, during Pakal's reign, Calakmul attacked and defeated Tikal in one of their many battles. The king of Tikal, Nun Bak Chak, escaped in AD 657 and fled to Palenque for refuge.[3] Palenque had also suffered from the military advances of Calakmul, having been successfully attacked in 599 and again in AD 611, Calakmul's king leading the last attack himself.[4]

Palenque's last king was Hanaab Pakal III, who acceded to the throne in AD 799. Not much is known about his reign, nor exactly how or when Palenque collapsed. Was it the result of war with neighboring superpowers? Was it a financial ruin, brought about by the overextension of the city's resources? Or was it a famine caused by overpopulation, deforestation, and the Mayan system of farming? We may never know for sure, but as with most ancient Mayan sites, it was probably a combination of several factors.

For many centuries, Palenque remained abandoned and forgotten, perhaps to all but a few local travelers who passed by it. Cortés apparently marched his army within 20 or 30 miles of the site without ever having realized it.[5] Because of rumors of fantastic ruins in the jungles of Chiapas; in the mid-18th century, expeditions were sent out from Guatemala City to investigate. Captain Antonio del Río explored it in 1787. The first drawings were made in 1807 during an expedition led by Guillermo Dupaix, who believed that the builders were from Atlantis. In 1832, the eccentric explorer Count Waldeck made extremely inaccurate and subjective drawings of the buildings and sculptures while living at the site.[6] Finally, Stephens and Catherwood's expedition in 1839 brought knowledge of Palenque's existence to the rest of the world with the publication of their ground-breaking travel diaries and highly accurate drawings a couple of years later.

The first photographs of Palenque were taken in 1858 by Désiré Charnay. Other famous archaeologists began to visit the site over the next decades, and the first major excavations began in 1934. That work has continued until today, but the most famous discovery began in 1949, when Alberto Ruz discovered that one of the stones of the floor of the Temple of Inscriptions was actually a sort of trapdoor leading down through rubble-filled tunnels to one of the greatest finds of the Mayan world: Pakal's tomb. In 2000, a project to map Palenque was completed, uncovering a total of 1,418 structures that compose the entire site! Not surprisingly, most of these remain unexcavated, but continuing archaeological work in some has uncovered a wealth of writings and artifacts that are adding to our understanding of this fascinating area.

## Ancient Names

Something else to look for that is not immediately apparent is the name itself: Lakamhá. It is well known that the current names of most ancient sites are not how they were known anciently. In some cases, we have no idea what they were called. It is interesting to note that the inhabitants named a city for the massive amount of water nearby, as Book of Mormon peoples may have used similar expressions. Cumorah is described as being in a land of many waters, rivers, and fountains. There are certainly areas of Mexico that match that description. When Lehi's group reached the sea, they gave it a name that meant "many waters." The Mayan ending of *ha* may be significant as well. Because of the need for water, the Maya built their cities near water sources, whether rivers, lakes, or sinkholes, as often as they could. In addition to Palenque, there are sites like Chichén Itzá, Cobá, and Yaxhá that follow this pattern. The ending of *ha* is not uncommon, either. Other ancient city names with this same ending are Lacanhá, Pusilhá, and Altunhá.

(continued on page 85)

*Can any support for the Book of Mormon be found in Pakal's tomb?*

for the next day. He did not know if he would be available, so we settled on a time of 11:30 at the stop in front of the hotel. If he could make it, great. If not, we would look for another bus back.

The hotel was a nice enough place. Although it was mainly a campground, they did have some thatched huts to stay in. These were comfortable, with lights, electricity, a locking door, and a decent bathroom with hot water. The staff, however, was not so friendly. They appeared to have the attitude of doing as little as possible and always seemed a bit put out when asked for something. The main desk was at the hotel restaurant where we had dinner. This particular evening, it was full of Europeans and hippies, and most of them were smoking. There was even musical entertainment: a guy playing guitar, panpipes, and singing. He was quite good, but one of the hippies (a man who looked too old to be slumming around the country for no apparent reason) decided that the music lacked something, so he jumped up next to the musician and began to accompany him on his own hand drum. The startled musician's response to this was to announce, "I guess I have percussion now," and then keep on playing.

The menu obviously catered to tourists, with some typically North American dishes alongside stereotypically Mexican ones. It was also translated into English, to make ordering a bit easier. The funny thing was that the translation was so bad, it was beyond atrocious. Inaccuracies

(continued on page 86)

# BRIEF SITE OVERVIEW

Notwithstanding the huge number of structures found here, relatively few are restored and open for tourists. What you can see is quite spectacular, though. As you walk down the path from the entrance, you will see a row of structures to your right, built up against a long, forested hill. The first one has the memorable name of Temple XII. Archaeologists' names for structures are seldom creative or descriptive, but their fascination with Roman numerals at Palenque just confuses the issue more. This building is also known as the Temple of the Skull or the Temple of the Dying Moon because of the stucco rabbit skull on its upper level.

Next to Temple XII is (no surprise) Temple XIII, which is not really much to look at. Next to that, however, is the Temple of the Inscriptions. This impressive pyramid and temple combination rises to a height of 200 feet. Its name comes from the multitude of hieroglyphs on the inner walls of the top structure. There are a total of 617 glyphs over three walls, the second-longest continuous Mayan inscription. They tell the story of Pakal's reign, the important events that happened during it, and his divine claim to power. We know that his son and heir, Kan Balam, finished the construction because the history ends with Pakal's death and the accession of his son to the throne.[7]

The floor of this building held the famous stone with 12 plugged holes that was lifted out by Alberto Ruz. After a couple of years of clearing out the rubble-filled passageway leading down, they opened the actual tomb of Pakal. The massive lid to his sarcophagus is unique and quite well known. Because of its size and the cramped quarters of the tomb, it still remains in place, while Pakal's skeleton and his sumptuous burial trove have been moved to the large anthropological museum in Mexico City.[8] Sadly, at the present time you cannot go down to the tomb, see the inscriptions, or even climb the pyramid. The entire structure is closed off to tourists. When we were there in January of 2007, we were told that the temple had been closed for four years while the experts try to figure out how to halt the deterioration of the hieroglyphs and stucco carvings. We spoke to several guards and a director at the museum and tried every excuse we could think of, but they would not let us in. From what we have seen of other sites and how notable structures become restricted, we would not be surprised if the general public were never allowed into the temple or the tomb again.

So far it had been raining nonstop without any sign of letting up. Not being able to seek shelter in the temple and wanting to get out of the rain, we headed toward the royal palace. In addition to the rivers, it rains at Palenque almost constantly, so unlike sites in the Yucatán, drought was never much of a concern here. Great Water indeed.

*(Ancient Names continued)* By comparison, there are place-names in the Book of Mormon that include this same suffix. Nephihah, Moronihah, Ammonihah, and Onihah are a few. What this suffix meant in the Nephite language is unclear, but it is seen in personal names as well. Thus Moronihah's name had some connection with his father's, Moroni. Since there was a land of Moron, Moroni's name may have meant that he was "from Moron." There was also a Jaredite king named Moron. He was wicked and ended up being overthrown and living in captivity, so perhaps he was aptly named. The fact that both a place and a person share a name is interesting, but it begs the question: which came first? In the case of Nephihah, it was most certainly named after one of the Nephis. There are other examples in the Book of Mormon of city founders naming the land after themselves. Even Moronihah was the name of both a person and a place. This happened in Mesoamerican history as well. Not only were lands and cities named after prominent leaders, but entire nations of people as well.[11]

and misspellings abounded, but our favorite was the *vaso de sangría*, which was rendered on the English section as a "glass of bleeding." Since *sangría* does not really translate, this unappetizing-sounding beverage was the result of confusing the drink's name with the English translation of the word *sangre*, Spanish for blood.

The rain continued off and on throughout the night and was still going strong in the morning. We did our best to prepare for a wet day, leaving our backpacks in the hut. Checkout time was at noon, so that was convenient for us. We caught a local van at the road in front of the hotel and were taken to the entrance of the site. There we paid our entrance fees and politely refused an offer from a nice young man who spoke English to be our guide. On the other side of the parking lot and entrance to the site, there were people setting up their booths to sell souvenirs. We neglected to buy anything at that time and later regretted it, because we ended up leaving Palenque at an entirely different spot, near the museum where there were no trinket vendors.

*At the Mayabell Campground, where you can get a hut to keep out of the rain and have a "glass of bleeding."*

If nothing else, the palace is a good place to get out of the rain. But it is also an amazing set of structures with many passageways and rooms to explore. The earliest rooms still visible are in the center of the whole structure, partly surrounding a courtyard in the northeastern corner. They were built during Pakal's reign. The tower, an unusual feature in Classic Mayan architecture, is definitely worth seeing. It was one of the later additions to the complex and may have served as a watchtower, an observatory, a sundial, or any combination of these. As with most monumental architecture, what is visible today is the sum of centuries of construction. In the courtyard are wonderful sculptures whose detail surpasses the usual bas-relief. It was originally believed that they represented tortured prisoners taken in war, but a more current idea is that they represent nobles or leaders from subject lands coming to offer tribute.[9] The faces are unique and so carefully crafted that they could indeed represent specific people.

Passing over to the other side of the palace, you will see an aqueduct built by the Maya that is still functional and filled with running water from the Otolum river. Mayan engineers used these combinations of natural features and human ingenuity to pipe water into the palace, giving it water pressure, six latrines, and two sweatbaths. Two of the toilets can be seen on the floor of the small courtyard to the south of the tower. In their heyday, these amenities rivaled any of the greatest Roman baths.

From this vantage point, you can walk down the steep steps to a path, cross over the aqueduct on a little bridge, and go to the Cross Group. This is a group of three temples completed by Pakal's son and dedicated in AD 692: the Temple of the Cross, the Temple of the Foliated Cross, and the Temple of the Sun. Thankfully, these structures have some meaningful names that make some sense. They are built upon artificial pyramids or platforms, although some are covered with so much vegetation that it is hard to tell. Visitors to the site can climb each of these to see the significant carvings inside. The doorways are gated and locked, but you can peer in to get a good look at the carvings. The only problem is that the reliefs are not very deep, so it is hard to see all the detail. Looking at drawings is a better way to really appreciate the imagery.

There is much more to Palenque, but these are the major structures that everyone visits. Because of its vast size and the number of buildings, you could spend days trying to see everything, although some areas are not open to tourists. A day should be sufficient to see the most important structures and get a good feel for the city, however. If you want to see more, you could take a path west from the parking lot and walk to a Mayan village and see the least visited areas of Palenque, or visit the museum. We definitely recommend that, since it contains one of the best collections of Mayan sculpture and artifacts, and admission is included in your ticket to enter the site.

To find the museum, take the path heading north from the palace. It winds through dense jungle and over some of Palenque's rivers, providing visitors with rewarding views of spectacular waterfalls. Keep following the path until you reach a paved road. This is the road leading into the site, so you have doubled back at this point. On the other side are the museum, a snack bar, some small shops, and offices.

## "And It Came to Pass"

Palenque is also mentioned in some LDS publications as containing carvings of a glyph meaning "and then it came to pass." There are ongoing Book of Mormon tours that visit the same sites we saw and cost thousands of dollars, not including the airfare. Some mention in their itineraries going to Palenque to climb the Temple of Inscriptions and look for the "it came to pass" glyph. If that is still their intention, we think they will be sorely disappointed upon arriving and discovering that the entire structure is indefinitely closed. We certainly were, but not for the same reason.

While we were very interested to read about the three examples in the Temple of Inscriptions from Joseph Allen's research,[12] we were even more excited from the results of our own studies that showed just how pervasive it really is in Mayan writings. While there are three examples of the *i-u-ti* and *u-ti-ya* glyphs on the west panel inside the temple, these are by no means the only ones you will

*The Temple of the Cross is another good place to look for the "it came to pass" glyph.*

find at Palenque. Incidentally, based on our comparisons with drawings made by Mayan scholars, we have concluded that the drawing that Allen uses in his book does not match up with accepted representations of this textual panel. Three glyphs are actually there on the west panel, but they do not correspond in location or variant to his illustration. The images we used for our comparison came from the acclaimed *Code of Kings* by Schele and Mathews, but they can be found in many well-known scholarly publications. The image Allen uses in *Exploring the Lands of the Book of Mormon* is actually from the right panel of the Temple of the Sun.

As at Yaxchilán, we have found that this glyphic phrase is all over the place. If a site has carved writing, it most likely has this glyph in there somewhere. It is so common and found at so many sites that we wonder why more LDS scholars are not mentioning it when dealing with linguistic similarities between the Book of Mormon and ancient Mesoamerican tongues. If they have found a few tantalizing examples at Palenque, why not all the rest?

*Drawing by Linda Schele, © David Schele, courtesy FAMSI, www.famsi.org*

To find this glyph in Palenque, you do have some other options. One is the Temple of the Cross. The main image is flanked by hieroglyphic panels on either side. On the left panel, an *u-ti-ya* glyph is in the second column from the right in the lower third of the text. On the right panel, an *i-u-ti* glyph is in the very bottom left corner of the text. These are not easy to see because of the indirect lighting and the shallow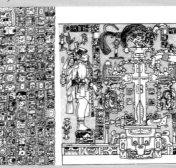

depth of the bas-relief, so an accurate drawing is your best bet to really make them out. Interestingly enough, because of the many different variations this glyph can take, we believe that the version in the right panel of this temple is the one Allen used as the primary illustration for this glyph in his book, even though he only mentions the Temple of Inscriptions as its location.

You can also find two examples in the Temple of the Foliated Cross. There is one in the right panel, third column from the left, in the row just above the bottom row. The *i-u-ti* phonetic components are stacked vertically in the left half of the glyph as opposed to taking up an entire glyphic square. We have seen this variation before at other sites. There is an *u-ti-ya* in the left panel as well, in the third column from the left, in about the bottom third of the panel.

Three examples can be found in the Temple of the Sun, all in the right panel of hieroglyphs. In the far right column, fourth and fifth rows down from the top, are an *u-ti-ya* and *i-u-ti*, respectively. Another *i-u-ti* can be found in the second column from the left, in the third row from the top. If the light is just right, you may be able to make these out by looking at the carving, but as always, an accurate drawing is the best way to really appreciate them.

For two really good examples of this glyph, just go to the excellent site museum. As you go through the door, turn right and head to the section on stone monuments. The very first one you come to is a stela with two columns of hieroglyphic text. Two of these glyphs are *i-u-ti*. They are large, beautifully carved, and impossible to miss if you know what you are looking for. Recent excavations in other structures such as Temple XIX and Building 2 of Group XVI at Palenque are yielding additional examples of this phrase in newly discovered carved texts.[13] From these many examples of text found at just one site, we realized that this phrase is just about as common in Mayan literature as it is in the Book of Mormon.

## Deities and the Sacred Tree of Life

The Cross Group is another must-see with important symbolism that escapes most visitors. These three temples were named by 19th-century explorers who thought that the cross shapes were Christian symbols. Modern archaeology has since disavowed this idea, claiming that the symbols represent the Mayan world tree instead. While this is essentially correct, the reverence the Maya had for this tree is similar in scope and meaning to the Christian world's veneration of the cross. The cultural origins of the world tree are unknown, but Mayan beliefs about it parallel quite closely some teachings in the Book of Mormon. That the tree is represented as a cross-like shape may or may not be coincidental.

The number of buildings in this group is not coincidental, however. While a dizzying array of gods and other deities were worshipped or acknowledged by the ancient Maya, Palenque is unique in that it had a special group of three gods known today as the Palenque Triad. Their exact nature is unknown, but they have to do with Palenque's mythical origins and creation. They are known to archaeologists simply as GI, GII, and GIII.[14] Their role in the creation is reflected in that in the Mayan view, the cosmos is formed by the placing of three great hearth-stones together. The world tree then grew in the interior space formed by them. These three temples represent the founding stones of creation as well as the three gods of the Palenque Triad.[15]

There is no agreement on the order or hierarchy of these temples, so we will start with the Temple of the Cross. The small structure at the top of the terraced pyramid ends in three rooms, very common in Mayan temples. In Palenque, these rooms are a place of purification, also represented by the Maya in their sweatbaths.[16] The middle room contains the carving of the cross-shaped tree. You cannot actually walk into the rooms, since they are blocked by gates, but you can get close enough to get a good look inside. The cross shape of the tree is immediately evident. It is growing out of a bowl that sits on a monstrous face. A bird is perched on top of the tree and a man is at either side. To some, these figures represent Pakal symbolically handing authority to his son, Kan Balam.[17] To others, both are Kan Balam, one as a youth and one as an adult.[18] This lack of agreement among archaeologists in interpreting images such as these in the Mayan world is not unusual at all. For every definite interpretation you find of a carving or structure, you can find another scholar's book with a completely different opinion.

This image has a particular connection with the carving on the lid to Pakal's tomb, one of the most famous Mayan carvings. While this wonderful sight is no longer available to the average visitor, it is well worth finding an image of it. A few decades ago, there was a fringe belief that the carving depicted Pakal at the controls of a spaceship, flying out to the stars. If you look at it horizontally and use a lot of imagination, you could perhaps get this impression. What significance this imagery has to a royal burial has not been adequately answered. Needless to say, mainstream archaeologists completely reject this hypothesis without a second thought. Notwithstanding the possibility of ancient astronauts, when the sarcophagus lid is compared to the back wall of the Temple of the Cross, it is obvious that the same cross-shaped object is depicted in both carvings and that it is definitely not a spaceship. As exciting as the thought of extra-terrestrial contact and Mayan space travel is, the real meaning behind this symbol and its purpose in a tomb and a temple is even more so, in our view.

For the deceased Pakal, the world tree is his pathway to the heavens. His unusual, curled-up position is not that of a space traveler in the cramped confines of a cockpit, but is symbolic of birth instead.[19] The tree then becomes a symbol

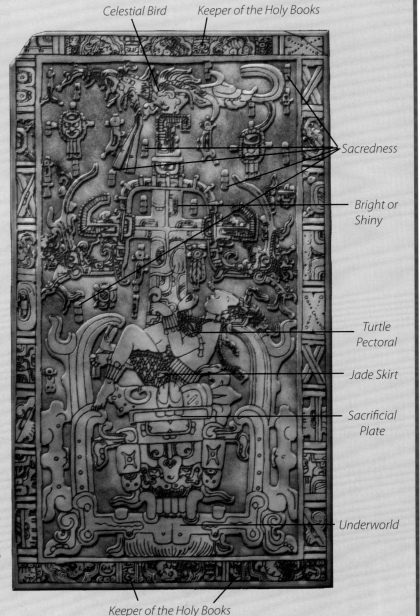

Celestial Bird

Keeper of the Holy Books

Sacredness

Bright or Shiny

Turtle Pectoral

Jade Skirt

Sacrificial Plate

Underworld

Keeper of the Holy Books

of rebirth after death, or resurrection. On the sides of the lid are carved figures of ten of his ancestors, emerging from cracks in the earth with flowering fruit trees, showing that they have passed through the same milestone. For each of these individuals, their deaths are recorded in Mayan as *och beh*, "he entered the road." In addition to the tree, the cracks represent resurrection as well, recalling the maize god who was killed by the lords of Xibalba, the Mayan underworld, then was reborn and emerged from a crack in the back of the cosmic turtle. As seen on the sides of this carving, the maize god's rebirth from this cleft is symbolized by the tree itself, so it is a direct symbol of resurrection. It is also interesting to note that the tree is thought of as being created from the sacrifice of a god.[20] On the lid of the sarcophagus, Pakal wears the beaded jade skirt of the maize god around his waist and a turtle pectoral on his chest, again reinforcing his belief in the resurrection.

The tree has mirror symbols on it, denoting it as shiny or bright. It is shown flowering and with a double-headed serpent wrapped around the crosspiece. The Maya called this tree *Wakah-Kan*, meaning "raised-up sky" for its role in the creation. *Kan* can also mean "serpent" in Mayan,[21] so perhaps the divine tree could also be referred to as "raised up serpent." In many Mesoamerican cultures, including the Olmec, Maya, and Aztec, serpents were a symbol of deity. Around the tree are symbols of *kulel,* or sacredness. The tree rises up from the quadripartite god, personifying a sacrificial plate for an offering. Below that are jaws opening into the underworld, Xibalba. The entire scene is framed with a skyband of celestial symbols, only a few of which are understood. Included in the skyband are some of Pakal's officials, two of whom carry the title *Ah Kul Hun*, meaning "keeper of the holy books."[22] One of them, Chak Kan, is shown twice: once on the top border, and once on the bottom.

Perched atop the tree is the celestial bird, a supernatural figure called Itzam-Ye or Mut-Itzamná. It is associated with or representative of a deity known as Itzamná. In the Yucatán, he was as close to a supreme deity as the Maya had. He was a creator god, placing the third hearthstone of creation. He is referred to with titles such as Lord and King, and is known for curing the sick. To him is attributed the invention of writing, and it is believed that he brought the arts of civilization to the people.[23] He is described as always benevolent and the son of or associated with a deity named Hunab Ku or Kinich Ahaw, known either as a supreme creator or god of the sun. Itzamná and Kinich Ahaw are sometimes depicted as bearded. In his curing abilities, his hands are given special attention and the sign of his hand was considered particularly holy. The Maya considered him to be the first priest. There used to be a temple dedicated to the healing hand of Itzamná located in the northern Yucatán town of Izamal, which was named for him.[24] Sadly, almost nothing remains of the ancient structures there, as it was taken apart and destroyed by the Spanish. It has been suggested that the Itzá Maya that settled in Chichén were named for him as well,[25] so this figure from their past has had a great deal of influence among them.

It is easy to see that this personage shares many characteristics with Quetzalcoatl. A very similar god was worshipped and known in Guatemala as Gukumatz. In fact, Quetzalcoatl, Kukulkan, and Gukumatz are merely the same name rendered in three of the different ancient languages of Mesoamerica.[26] The same could be said about Viracocha in Peru. It might be asked why there are so many gods with Christlike attributes. We are not trying to equate any one of these deities with Jesus Christ directly, but there may be a common source for these different beings. Far from being a unified people and culture, the Maya were disparate peoples, living in many separate regions with distinct languages and customs. Certain traits were shared, like the calendar, writing, and major deities, but there were local customs particular to the different groups. The Yucatec Maya were apparently already worshipping Itzamná when the Toltecs arrived, bringing Quetzalcoatl with them.

Another point to keep in mind is the nature of Mayan supernatural beings, which were unlike their counterparts in the mythologies of the Middle East. Although the Maya had over 250 names for their deities, these should not all be thought of as separate and distinct beings. They viewed their gods with a degree of fluidity; each god could take on different manifestations or characteristics. They viewed them as having dual natures, able to take on opposite qualities. Another belief was that each god existed in four forms, each aspect relating to a cardinal direction.[27] Thus, the complexity of the Mayan pantheon is a bit difficult for our modern culture to understand, with several different gods sharing similar descriptions or traits and the same deity being described differently at various times. If Jesus Christ's visit was remembered and passed on by different people in ancient America, we should not be surprised to see his attributes in various local deities from these areas.

The world tree, however, seemed to be a universally shared concept. The Maya saw it as the axis mundi, or center of the world and creation with the three hearthstones around it. It rose straight up from the ground and held the sky up with branches that ran out from the trunk at right angles toward the four cardinal directions. It was a conduit from the mortal world down to the underworld and up to the heavens. Since Itzamná's symbol dwelt in its branches, the path to the heavens and a divine afterlife led through him. The Maya probably derived these details from their real-world example of this sacred tree, the ceiba.[28] These native trees are smooth and light in color, rising up vertically to heights of 175 feet or more. The branches do not begin until near the top, so they seem to exist far above the ground, holding up the very sky itself.

Another famous example of a carved tree that is of particular interest to Latter-day Saints is on Stela 5 in Izapa. For decades, some LDS writers have theorized that this carving depicts not only the tree of life as mentioned in the Book of Mormon, but a detailed account of Lehi's dream from 1 Nephi chapter 8 in particular.[29] It should go without saying that mainstream archaeologists do not share this view. While its exact interpretation remains elusive, its suggested representations range from a creation scene to a marketplace. Agreeing with an LDS perspective would almost certainly be professional suicide for any Mayan expert, member or not, so we should not expect that. It may very well have been carved by someone familiar with Lehi's dream, or it may have nothing to do with the Book of Mormon. Its time period and location do fit in with what we would expect. From an LDS point of view, it may make perfect sense, but those who think that are alone in their interpretation.

Pakal's sarcophagus is an entirely different matter. The interpretation of the varied elements in this image is almost universally agreed upon in modern archaeology; there is nothing controversial in what we have described. Yet this piece is replete with doctrinal symbolism that could have come straight out of the Book of Mormon. In the same way that the apostate Christian world adopted the cross as its supernal symbol of hope, the Maya could have appropriated the scriptural Tree of Life, being unfamiliar with the cross of the Old World. This life-giving tree, perhaps present from the beginning in the Garden of Eden, was known to our first parents and seen by Book of Mormon prophets as representing the love of God, his greatest gift to mankind. For the later Mayan peoples, it could have come to symbolize all that they hoped for as they passed from this world to the next: eternal life and becoming divine.

The same major symbols seen on Pakal's sarcophagus lid are found on the wall of the Temple of the Cross. The sacred tree rises up from a sacrificial plate, reaching up from the underworld monster at the base to the heavenly Itzam-Ye bird at the top of its branches. A band at the base of the image carries similar celestial symbols to those found in Pakal's sarcophagus frame. The two figures on either side of the tree represent Kan Balam's authority and accession to the throne, whether both images are of him or one is his father. Mayan kings were anxious to associate themselves with this symbol as a sign of their power and right to kingship, as evidenced by the lintel at Yaxchilán, which shows a smaller and simplified version of the world tree and celestial bird. Other sites we visited, such as Copán, show royal monuments of the kings employing these same symbols as images of their divine right to rule and connection to the gods.

The pyramid on which this temple stands has a base built around the proportions of the golden mean. The Maya used this geometrical principle in the construction of their structures. The proportions of their buildings, inside and out, were very important to them. Similar to artists of the Old World, they saw these proportions in nature and wished to bring their sacred and profane structures into harmony with it. Mayan builders used measured lengths of cord to transform a square into this perfect rectangle, mimicking the act of creation as carried out by the gods. They imagined the creator gods measuring and laying out the cosmos with celestial cords to create a rectangle, extending out to the four directions[30] with the world tree in the center.

Next is the Temple of the Foliated Cross. The imagery is very similar, with the world tree represented as a flowering stalk of corn, or maize. This is an even more direct allusion to the maize god and to corn itself, also thought of by the Maya as being divine because of the crucial role it played in their culture.[31] The symbolic importance of corn permeated every aspect of Mayan existence, from the creation, through mortal life, and beyond the grave. The sacrifice and resurrection of the maize god created the tree that lifted up the heavens and exposed the mortal world. They believed that people in this phase of creation were created from a mixture of maize dough and the blood of the gods.[32] This is why the need for sacrifice was so great among the Maya: they owed a debt of blood to the gods and had to pay it back. Corn was the primary food item in their diet, a literal as well as spiritual bread of life. Finally, in the next life, mankind could follow the path of the maize god and be reborn, heading up the world tree, passing the celestial bird into the heavens.

On the left of the tree, Kan Balam wears the beaded jade skirt of the maize god, just like his father. This may represent his divine authority derived from the maize god, as well as his eventual resurrection after death. The tree is surrounded by similar symbols of sacredness as on Pakal's tomb cover. There is no offering plate or quadripartite god this time, the tree growing instead from a water lily monster, symbolizing both the underworld of Xibalba and the watery fields in which maize was grown.[33] Some of the text refers to the birth of the god GII of the Palenque triad.[34] Other glyphs recount Kan Balam's accession to the throne.

The depiction of the world tree as a stalk of corn in this temple illustrates these important roles that maize played in the Mayan world. Heads sprout from its leaves on either side. This could recall the belief that when he was killed in the ball court of the underworld, the maize god's head was hung in a nearby tree.[35] Thus, the image of a tree figures into the death as well as the resurrection of this god. Just how the maize god fit in with other deities is currently not fully understood. He has been connected with GI of the Palenque triad, who also had a rebirth or resurrection, then ascended to the heavens.[36] His resurrection began the creation of the cosmos, and his divine tree is believed to be the center of everything.

From the examples we have mentioned, there seems to be no quick and easy way to connect a singular Mesoamerican deity with Jesus Christ. The same personage is known by different names in different cultures and seemingly different gods share some common Christlike attributes. The unusual flexibility with which the Maya viewed their gods only confuses the issue more to modern students. The truth is that so much of ancient Mayan thought has been lost that we may never know exactly how they worshipped. However, new research can shed some light on their beliefs that can bring about a partial understanding. Not all of this is universally accepted, but here are very reasonable assertions about important Mayan deities, based on the latest archaeological studies:

1. The maize god was sacrificed in the underworld and his resurrection created the tree that started the current creation cycle and leads to the heavens and resurrection.

2. GI of the Palenque triad had a resurrection and his ascent to the heavens happened "under the auspices of Itzamná."[37] The date of this event is recorded in the Temple of the Cross and because this date (9 Wind) is also a name for Quetzalcoatl, he may be a local counterpart to this deity.[38] GI is also a principal creator god.

3. Itzamná is a major deity and creator god whose symbol appears in the maize god's tree. He is known for his benevolence, healing hands, and giving the arts of civilization.

4. Quetzalcoatl, Kukulkan, and Gukumatz all refer to the same individual, originally a benevolent god symbolized by the feathered serpent, who gave peaceful and uplifting teachings to the people. Additionally, we believe that Itzamná could refer to this same being as well, because of his similar attributes.

While there may never be definite proof, it is easy to see that teachings from Book of Mormon prophets about the Savior could have been the source for all of these deities. Why they ended up being expressed in different gods could be explained by the fluid Mayan concept of divinity and the fact that Mesoamerica contains distinct cultural groups that have evolved isolated from each other in some aspects. Original teachings could have been interpreted and implemented differently by different groups. The lasting impact of Jesus' visit to this continent could have filtered down through the ages to these groups who ended up with a fragmentary understanding of his doctrines and attributes, embodied in their local gods.

# TIKAL

local spider monkey

date on Stela 29

stela and altar grouping

# How We Got There

At around noon, after spending half a day touring Palenque, we waited at the entrance of the site for a local bus to take us back to our hotel and into town. From the main town of Palenque we planned on finding a bus at the terminal that would take us back to Corozal. Not two minutes later Luis, the driver who had originally taken us to Palenque, drove by in his empty van. We did not realize it at the time, but we were within walking distance of our hotel. He said he had been driving around looking for us. We were quite pleased with our good luck and piled in. He then told us the price: 700 pesos, more than what we had paid the day before. We had been told that a bus ride to Corozal should not be that much, but he was under the impression that we had an agreement and now that we were the only passengers, he must have felt he had to make more profit from each of us. Eventually, we got him to lower the price to 600, but only after hours of conversation along the way. Again, this was an instance in which being able to communicate in the language was beneficial.

From Palenque, Luis took the main freeway 199 down to Frontera Corozal. Our 171-km trip took approximately two and a half hours and was a

(continued on page 100)

98

## BACKGROUND

There is some debate over Tikal's name and what it means. One translation gives it the meaning "place of spirits," another "place of the count of Katun."[1] Although there are some experts that believe Tikal is the original name, it appears that the general consensus among archaeologists is that its original Classic-period name was Mutul, meaning "knot of hair."[2] The fact that the emblem glyph shows the rear view of a human head with a knot tied on it seems to confirm this translation. The earliest known use of this emblem glyph was in AD 376 and is found on Stela 39.[3] In the seventh century, a site now known as Dos Pilas began using the same emblem glyph, perhaps under the authority of Tikal, which began to be called Yax Mutul, or "First Mutul."[4] The smaller Mutul eventually defected and allied itself with Tikal's archrival Calakmul.

Ceramic evidence shows that Tikal was inhabited at least as far back as 900 BC[5] and the site was inhabited for close to 2,000 years.[6] The city covers about 65 square kilometers with 3,000 structures covering the site and an estimated 10,000 structures

remaining buried under ground.[7] At one point the population of the city peaked from between 100,000 to 200,000 people, although there are arguments that this figure is much higher.[8] Some archaeologists have argued that the "slash and burn" farming techniques known among the Maya could not have sustained such a large population density and that more highly advanced farming techniques must have been employed at the site.[9]

The earliest date carved at the site is AD 292 and is found on Stela 29, a monument that celebrates a ruler named Foliated Jaguar.[10] The dynastic founder of Tikal is named First Step Shark or Yax Chaktel Xok, and he reigned until around AD 200, after which hieroglyphic texts tell us that there were 31 rulers, 16 of whom are known by emblem glyph today.[11] True Great Jaguar Claw (Toh Chak Ich Ak) was one of the greatest of Tikal's kings and ruled for 61 years.[12] Although we do not know when he became king, we do know that he died in AD 378, the day of his victory over their major rival at the time, Uaxactún.[13] True Great Jaguar Claw's death and victory are recorded on Stela 31 at Tikal.[14]

## BOOK OF MORMON COMPARISONS

*Tikal lies within what are most likely Book of Mormon lands. It was inhabited before the arrival of Lehi's group and has a very long history. Who the first inhabitants were is unknown, but the time and place match up and there are some notable similarities.*

### Ongoing Warfare

Tikal was involved in many wars throughout its history. In the early Classic, nearby Uaxactún was a serious rival until it was defeated and subjugated. Their wars and more particularly Tikal's victories are recorded on monuments at the site. For much of the mid-Classic period, its arch-enemy was the more distant kingdom of Calakmul. The near constant warfare between the two superpowers spread to much of the surrounding region as most smaller sites took sides in the conflict. Centuries of fighting eventually depleted resources at both sites, but Tikal emerged as the victor.

Hostilities began between Nephites and Lamanites before the first generation of Lehi's group had passed away and continued off and on for much of the Book of Mormon's history, except for a period of time following the Savior's visit. The length of the conflict and the resulting battles seemed difficult to place into Mesoamerican history, especially when the dominant scholarly opinion for much of the 20th century was that there was not warfare of this kind in the Mayan area. What we know of the history between Tikal and its enemies shows that the many battles depicted in the Book of Mormon are plausible.

different experience than our trip up. Having the van to ourselves, we had more space to sleep and opportunity to talk to Luis. We spent much of the trip talking about life in Mexico and comparing it to life in the United States, which proved to be very educational and interesting. Conversations with locals like Luis throughout our trips were often rewarding.

Luis dropped us off at the river's edge where boats waited to take travelers up and down the river to local sites and to cross the border. The place was crowded with boats so we easily secured a boat and agreed on payment to take us to Co-op Bethel. Despite the beautiful surroundings, we grew anxious on the boat as we neared the town, for the moment of truth had arrived. In what kind of condition would we find our rental car after a day and night at Milton and Ludi's home? Would our car even be there when we arrived? All we had was a stranger's promise that it would be safe. Our boat took us to what appeared to be our original castoff point. The only problem was that the boatmen now wanted more money, but we firmly reminded them of the previously agreed upon price.

After paying, we quickly walked up the hill and back to our car, finding it in exactly the same condition we left it. We were greeted by Ludi (Señor Brillones's daughter) who refused to be paid for watching our car, even after we offered several times. Considering the hospitality she had shown us, it did not seem right not to pay

(continued on page 102)

100

The conflict between these cities is evidenced from writing found at both cities and a fortified trench and embankment protecting Tikal's northern border.[15] To the people of Tikal, True Great Jaguar Claw was one of the greatest leaders to have ever lived. He was their national hero, and his memory was treated like that of George Washington in the United States. Located in the central acropolis, the building dedicated to his name remained unchanged for over 500 years as later kings built their shrines and tombs around his for hundreds of years.[16] This building was considered one of the holiest of places in Tikal, not only by those that lived there, but even by enemies who left this building alone while they destroyed other monuments in the city.[17]

After Uaxactún, Calakmul became the next major rival to Tikal. The two cities thrived economically and grew to be the two major superpowers in the Mayan world, each with its own allied cities in the surrounding regions. In AD 659, Shield Skull (Nuun Ujol Chaak), the king of Tikal, took refuge with his ally Pakal at Palenque after he was defeated by Calakmul.[18] Thirteen years later, Shield Skull returned to take back his throne and was successful. Unfortunately for him, his victory was short-lived. Seven years later Calakmul, along with its ally Dos Pilas, attacked Tikal and won, sacrificing Shield Skull on May 3, 679.[19] From the historical evidence it appears that there was a massive amount of casualties in this war with important monuments and records from the previous 200 years being destroyed by the victors.[20]

Tikal had important contacts that stretched beyond the Mayan world. Like Calakmul, it controlled important trade roots in the area, creating imported wealth for the city. Tikal's connection to Teotihuacán in central Mexico is evidenced by similar ceramics and examples of green obsidian that can only be found at Teotihuacán.[21] Some experts have even suggested that at least one of Tikal's rulers, Spearthrower Owl, came from Teotihuacán.[22]

Although Tikal eventually ended up on the winning end of its conflicts with Calakmul, its glory and power were not to last. Internal troubles began to overwhelm the city during the ninth century. The last carved date found at Tikal is AD 892.[23] Its downfall followed the same general pattern of decline that occurred in the Petén and elsewhere in the southern Lowlands and remains a mystery as well as a point of debate among scholars.[24] What we do know is that the focus of Mayan civilization began shifting northward at this time and would peak for the next few centuries in the Yucatán.

By 1847, descriptions of Tikal were appearing in Guatemalan periodicals. Modesto Méndez was perhaps the first official visitor to the site, led there by Ambrosio Tut, governor of San José.[25] He was a government official at the time, and his works were published in Berlin a year later. It is interesting that Stephens and Catherwood did not hear about Tikal and never visited or mentioned it on their expedition through Guatemala, even though they traveled extensively through Mesoamerica, seeking any news of ancient ruins. Considering the many smaller sites they visited and documented, they would certainly have made their way to Tikal had they heard any rumor about it. Archaeological study of Tikal has been extensive, perhaps more so than any other Mayan site.[26] Between 1956 and 1969, the University of Pennsylvania and the Guatemalan government completed much

## Defensive Earthworks

While not seen by the average visitor to Tikal, 2.8 miles north of the city center is a defensive system of earthworks, consisting of a wall and trench that span east to west for at least six miles.[50] It is thought that this fortification was built during the early Classic period, which begins around AD 250. At 19 feet tall from the bottom of the trench to top of the mound, this would have been a formidable barrier to rival cities. There was most likely a wooden wall or palisade running along the top. There are corresponding earthworks to the south of the city as well.[51] Tikal is also protected to the west and east by large areas of low, swampy land, called bajos, that would have been extremely difficult for an invading force to pass through.

The timing of these massive earthworks coincides with the end of the Book of Mormon when war was becoming increasingly widespread and Tikal was not the only such fortified city. Others in the Petén region had similar earthworks, and this kind of defensive construction is seen in this region and northward up to Becán, perhaps the most famous example. Calakmul, Tikal's most bitter rival, had huge defensive walls made of stone instead of earth, but they evidence the same need. In Alma chapters 49 and 50, Captain Moroni fortifies many cities against Lamanite attack, using a system of earthworks that appear to be the same as those discovered by archaeologists. Although the wars during

(continued on page 103)

her, so again we offered. We told her to take 100 pesos as a gift, which she eventually did. It was late afternoon and our time was running out so we loaded up our SUV. Noticing a grapefruit tree

on the way out, we asked if she had any that we could buy for drinking *mate* (an Argentine herbal tea). She brought a bucket full of them back to us, offering them for free.

We stopped back at Señor Brillones's shop to say good-bye and change our remaining pesos back into quetzals. After a quick stop at the immigration building on the outskirts of town, we were on our way. Overall we felt lucky to have covered so much ground and been treated so well by the people in Bethel.

We drove out from Bethel on the same rough, rocky road we had taken in two nights before. Before long, we reached Highway 5 and turned left to Flores, then turned northward to Tikal. Bus rides from Bethel to Flores are supposed to take four hours, but we made it all the way to Tikal in about two and a half hours. We arrived just after nightfall, parking at the campsite that was located near the entrance to the site. The

(continued on page 104)

of the restoration work, under field director Edwin M. Shook. In the early 1980s, the Lost World complex was excavated by archaeologists working under Guatemala's anthropological institute. In some areas, the work still appears to be ongoing. Nonetheless, the common saying by guides at the site was that only about 20 percent of Tikal has been excavated.

The excavation of tombs and study of artifacts at Tikal have provided important insights into the Mayan world. Many royal tombs have been discovered at the site, filled with jade artifacts, shells, obsidian, and other important offerings. These tombs rival those of Egypt, although archaeologists have made a point to avoid such direct comparisons. One particular item worth noting is Pot G3 discovered at Hasaw Kan Kawil's tomb. This Mayan king was another very important leader whose reign brought a major defeat to Calakmul and a resurgence of strength at Tikal. The pot from his tomb depicts a tribute scene showing the presentation of cloth and other objects by lords who hold the title of *Ah Kul Hun* or "keeper of the holy books."[27]

## BRIEF SITE OVERVIEW

We were surprised to discover that unlike any other site we visited, Tikal can be entered at practically any hour. Even in the middle of the night, visitors can wander around the site and

tour its structures, accompanied by local guards, some of whom carry shotguns. We considered doing this, but we did not really have the time, and sleep seemed like a better idea. We arranged for a guide the night we arrived to take us early in the morning to Temple IV to see the sunrise. We figured this would allow us to get an early start on touring such a large site and possibly provide us with a spectacular view undefiled by hoards of tourists. Without a guide to take you in the early morning, you have to wait until the park officially opens at 6:00 a.m. What we did not count on is that this is a very popular activity here and we were among a sizable group of people.

With the other tourists, we walked toward Temple IV in the darkness of early morning. Once we arrived to the base of the temple, we climbed some very steep wooden stairs to the top and waited for the sun to rise. We were lucky to be among the first there because as time passed, the entire area on the top of the temple filled with people. We had not experienced crowds like this at any other Mayan site and figured it would only get worse. As you can see, there is no getting in early to avoid the rush, but at least we had a decent spot on the top of the pyramid. So many people enter Tikal in the wee hours and climb to the tops of accessible temples that timing is crucial

(*Defensive Earthworks continued*) his time were fought a century or two before most of these fortifications now known, the similarity is striking, and it is possible that the Maya built them based on previous examples. It is also interesting that most of these fortified cities are in the same region, which probably corresponds to the northeastern boundaries of Nephite lands. With many of them being inhabited during Preclassic times, it is possible that evidence of some Nephite defenses has survived to this day.

# Right Time and Place

Although most of what is visible today dates too far after the close of the Book of Mormon, there are some structures that had their beginnings during Book of Mormon times. The two earliest areas of Tikal's visible construction are the Lost World Complex and the North Acropolis. Both were built during Preclassic times, and additions continued to be built throughout the ensuing centuries. While the bulk of known history at Tikal is from the Classic period, unlike many other sites, its surviving record stretches back to the end of the Preclassic era. Still, archaeological evidence shows that there was activity here long before the written record begins.

Ceramic evidence indicates that this area was settled centuries before the beginning of Nephite history, but the founding of Tikal is generally thought to have occurred around 600 BC.[52] By this time, groups of people living in structures of perishable materials had

(continued on page 105)

campsite was basically a grassy field next to a local restaurant. The ground was already wet, and it looked like it was going to rain.

Compared to another night out in the elements, the local hotels looked especially tempting considering all the traveling we had been through that day, so once again we decided to give in and stay at one of the nicer hotels right near the park called the Tikal Inn, paying US $60 for a room, our most expensive lodgings yet. The rooms there were basic, but overall very nice. There was a pool, restaurant, and Internet access that allowed us to quickly send some email home. We hurried to shower and enjoy the services before everything went dark at 10:00 p.m. when the electricity was turned off for the night.

*And it is even steeper than it looks.*

to getting a good spot. We could have gone to another structure, but Temple IV seemed a good choice. It is a must-see for *Star Wars* fans because the view looking east with the tops of Temples I and II poking above the trees was used as the backdrop for the rebel base at the end of the first movie, *A New Hope*.

At 231 feet tall, Temple IV is the tallest building at the site and may be the tallest structure in all of the ancient New World.[28] It was built by Yikin Chan Kawil, who some experts believe lies buried in a tomb deep within the temple.[29] His name has been difficult to translate, but one interpretation is that it means "Darkness of the Night Sky."[30] The views from the top of this giant temple are spectacular. From our vantage point we could see many of the large, important temples at Tikal along with a vast jungle forest that was teeming with life. The sunrise was a bit of a letdown though, due to the haze and clouds, which are often present at this site. There was no glorious daybreak of the sun over the forest canopy; the overcast sky simply got lighter and lighter until we knew the sun had to be up somewhere.

After sunrise we climbed down the long wooden staircase and headed toward the Lost World complex. As we walked rain began to pour down on us, continuing on and off (mostly on) for the remainder of our visit to Tikal. As we entered the Lost World complex we got a sense for how it got its name. The place has a very ancient feel to it. The original explorers gave this section the name based on Conan Doyle's book *The Lost World* because they felt it perfectly captured the atmosphere of the story.[31] The base of the central pyramid measures 264 feet and rises to a height of 100 feet.[32] Ceramics found under the Lost

World Pyramid have been dated to between 800 and 600 BC. The structure dates back to the late Preclassic period, its first phase of construction ending at around 500 BC, with later constructions overlying it.[33] It is believed that the pyramid served as an observatory for recording astronomical events and seasons.[34]

After climbing the Lost World Pyramid and enjoying the views at the top, we descended and headed toward Temple V. On our way we passed through the Plaza of the Seven Temples, a place that some experts believe serves as a transitional space that divides the ceremonial from public space.[35] From here the narrow trail took us through some heavily forested areas where we saw colorful parrots and other wildlife before the vegetation opened up and Temple V came into view.

(*Right Time and Place continued*) settled here. Their origin and what they called themselves or their settlement are unknown.[53] Tikal's first ruling dynasty dates back to the second century BC, but again, little is known about that time period. Between AD 200 and 400, ritual and dynastic life here changed and became more dynamic and complex.[54]

Few of the original structures have been kept pristine, but some very early construction can still be seen. The initial Lost World Pyramid was built by 200 BC and was completed by about AD 1, becoming one of the most massive structures in America at the time.[55] The structures in this area are thought to commemorate the passage of the sun and cycles of time. The North Acropolis was used for important burials from very early in Tikal's history, starting around 350 BC. It began to take on its current visible arrangement in about AD 250.[56] The Great Plaza between Temples I and II has four layers of plaster floors; the earliest dates back to 150 BC.[57] It is rare to be able to appreciate so much early architecture in a Mayan Classic city. Most of what is visible

(continued on page 107)

*The Lost World Pyramid, which dates to well within Book of Mormon times.*

The rain returned at this point, so we took refuge under a thatched covering just in front. There we had time to eat some snacks and read about the history of this imposing structure. Temple V has only recently been restored. To get to the top you must climb some unusually steep (and now slick) wooden stairs on the side of the temple, which with the addition of rain made for an intimidating and heart-pounding climb. It stands at 190 feet and the stairway is more like a ladder, so if you have a fear of heights, you may want to skip this one. We made the climb up during a break in the rain and rested at the top, trying to catch our breath. At the top is a single room with massive exterior walls that is closed off to the public. It is believed by some experts that this temple was built by Ruler C (Yax Ain II), who ascended to the throne in AD 768.[36]

From Temple V we walked to the Great Plaza. This is one of the most famous areas in the Mayan world, and for good reason. The unique and iconic structures surrounding it have been photographed many times and are instantly recognizable. Standing in the middle of the Great Plaza, if you face directly north, you see the North Acropolis with its many ancient tombs and temples. To your left is Temple II, to your right is Temple I, and directly behind you is the Central Acropolis. The entire area was an important ceremonial place dating back to the Preclassic era. There are circular altars on the ground that are still used by the local Maya for burning copal resin in ceremonies. Many of the monuments lining the plaza were put back by later inhabitants, so their original locations have been lost. Some were even reinstalled upside down.

The rain was still coming down, so we tried to find a covered spot among the modern thatched roofs that cover important excavated areas. We first walked to the North Acropolis, an area that is credited as one of earliest settlement places in Tikal.[37] Ceramics found buried here date to between 800 and 600 BC.[38] Development of the North Acropolis began around 350 BC and served as a burial place for important rulers of Tikal. Passing the mostly blank and unimpressive stelae that are so numerous they almost act as a fence to the temples, we walked up the stairs in search of the temples and tombs of True Great Jaguar, Curl Snout, Stormy Sky, Animal Skull, and other past kings of Tikal. Many important artifacts have been found buried in tombs here that have greatly

contributed to our understanding of the Maya. Unfortunately, these discoveries came at a price. Archaeologists dismantled many of the later temples during their excavation work in the North Acropolis.[39] This "renovation" has left the North Acropolis somewhat plain, and we were slightly disappointed that there was not a lot to see, except a row of partial temples and buildings. Of all the buildings here, the most important is probably True Great Jaguar's tomb, found in the center of the North Acropolis.

From the North Acropolis we walked toward Temple II and climbed more steep wooden stairs to the top. This temple was built at some point during Sky Rain's (Jasaw Chan Kawil)

(*Right Time and Place continued*) from the plaza, however, such as the temples, Central Acropolis, and the later shrines of the North Acropolis, is from the Classic era.

This area of Guatemala, known as the Petén, probably corresponds to the East Wilderness of the Book of Mormon. There are many other sites in this remote area and most date back to Book of Mormon times, even the great Classic kingdom of Tikal. With similar defensive fortifications as those used by the Nephites, sites in this region may have seen some of the wars mentioned in the Nephite record. The time and place of ancient settlements here match Book of Mormon geography, so we look with anticipation as more insights emerge about Preclassic history here.

## Destruction of Records

Texts recording 200 years of history were destroyed after major defeats suffered by Tikal in the late seventh century. One of the worst defeats was at the hands of Calakmul in AD 679 where experts believe many of Tikal's residents were slaughtered.[58] What little we do know comes from surviving texts carved in the Classic era, long after the end of the Book of Mormon. This tendency to destroy the records of rival cities defeated in conquest was commonplace not just in the Mayan region, but throughout much of Mesoamerica. Were it not for the loss of these records, much more could be known about earlier periods of history.

(continued on page 109)

reign, which began in AD 682.[40] It is believed by some archaeologists that Sky Rain built Temple II in dedication to his wife.[41] From the top of the temple we faced the 154-foot tall Temple I, which was built for Sky Rain and served as his tomb. Experts are not sure if he completed it before his death or if his son completed the construction after his father's death.[42] Sky Rain's tomb was discovered in 1962 as a result of tunneling excavations and was full of jade, pearl, and shell jewelry along with many other important artifacts. Some experts believe that Sky Rain, like the Egyptians and Pakal the Great of Palenque, planned and began building Temple I in preparation for his own death.[43] As an ally, it is possible that Sky Rain knew Pakal of Palenque, who also had his own funerary pyramid, and attended his funeral.

Sadly, climbing the steps to the top of Temple I is not allowed. They are so smooth and worn (not to mention slippery in the rain) and their angle is so steep that we are not sure it would even be remotely safe anymore. In fact, we did not climb the original steps of any of the major temples at Tikal. The only way visitors are permitted to scale their heights is on a modern series of wooden ladders and platforms. After descending from Temple II's platform, we walked southward and up a few stairs to a collection of many smaller buildings and complexes called the Central Acropolis. The best way to get through this maze of more functional buildings is with the help of a detailed site map. Construction began here in the late Preclassic period and continued until the collapse of Tikal, a period lasting almost 1,200 years.[44] A small ballcourt separates the Central Acropolis from Temple I. The structures here had many different functions that have been difficult to identify. Some suggestions have ranged from varying rooms serving as family residences of the elite to ceremonial houses and courts. There is some belief that some spaces were set aside for religious ceremonies and have been compared to royal chapels.[45]

Leaving the Central Acropolis, we walked through Group G and onto a trail that, after a long walk, led us to Temple VI or The Temple of Inscriptions, which like Temple IV was built by Darkness of the Night Sky.[46] Measuring 80 feet tall, this temple was the last discovered large temple at Tikal. There are three doorways at the top of the temple and a 40-foot roof comb that on its back side contains the longest block of text at the site.[47] The inscriptions have recorded dates that cover a span of 1,905 years and begin at 1139 BC.[48] The meaning of much of the text is a mystery, but it is believed that the early text deals with early historical events. The later writing is about the life and achievements of Darkness himself. The last date on the inscriptions is AD 766.[49]

On our way out, we stopped to see one of Tikal's twin-pyramid complexes. There are seven at the site, labeled Complexes L through R. Each one was built and dedicated at the end of a katun, a period of time in the Mayan calendar consisting of 20 of their years. They are only known in this area of the Petén, but archaeologists can only speculate as to their true significance and function. We also stopped at the site museum before leaving Tikal. There we found the oldest carved date known in the Mayan Lowlands on Stela 29. Its Long Count date corresponds to AD 292, but with amusement we noted that the plaque describing the Mayan date had some of the numbers wrong. Unfortunately, the caretaker did not want any pictures taken inside and was very strict about this policy. There was someone watching us everywhere we went. But there are some beautiful artifacts and exhibits there, so we suggest taking a look. In addition to Stela 29, there are also some interesting pottery, tools, worked obsidian, and a tomb reconstruction that have been discovered at the site.

We could have spent two days exploring the ruins of Tikal; it is just that large. But there was a downside to our experience. The lack of legible inscriptions and well-preserved stelae, added to the near constant rain, were somewhat of a disappointment. And there was a rather unpleasant experience involving vicious ants crawling up our pant legs. Our recommendation is to keep far away from any trails of ants that you might see. However, we cannot think of any other site that gives the visitor a greater sense of what a great Mayan city would have been like during ancient times. Near the entrance are some open-air shops that are a good source for replicas, books, and local handicrafts. They are situated around some large ponds where signs are posted, warning of crocodiles. We were told that any sizable body of water in these areas could harbor these large reptiles, and remembering the ones we saw on the Usumacinta River, we did not linger near the water's edge too long.

(*Destruction of Records continued*) Early in Nephite history, Enos implores the Lord to protect their records from the Lamanites in Enos 13–14. Almost 1,000 years later, Moroni, the last Nephite record keeper, had to flee northward to protect the sacred record, even though the Nephites had been destroyed and he was but one man. We see the Lamanites following practices that were common among the Maya. Considering all the records that have been destroyed from the beginning of Mesoamerican history to the Spanish occupation, it is no wonder that Nephite records have not been found.

# Wars of Conquest

Through the tireless efforts of Mayan epigraphers like Heinrich Berlin and Tatiana Proskouriakoff, we now know that warfare was an intrinsic part of Mayan culture. A common justification for these wars is that they were to capture victims for sacrifice.[59] Often, wars were timed to coincide with astronomical events to gain protection from the gods.[60] But something was about to change. On January 16, AD 378, the Tikal king Great Jaguar Paw fought a different kind of war against nearby Uaxactún. Unlike previous wars, this date had no astronomical significance,[61] and the attack appeared to be solely for the purpose of conquest and expansion. How did this change in the practice of war come about? Since the first century AD, there was interaction between Tikal and Teotihuacán, a city known for its violent imagery and conquests. The Maya likely borrowed this martial imagery (and idea) of conquest war from Teotihuacán and incorporated it into their own culture.[62] This was not the first or the last time the Maya would borrow ideas from other cultures and make them their own. Those interested in Teotihuacán and the Toltecs should study up on Chichén Itzá, something we plan to do in the future.

This new kind of war may have been part of a new age of violence. The end of the Preclassic period around AD 250 ended with cities abruptly being depopulated or abandoned altogether and cultural development ceasing for a time. The archaeological record suggests that widespread warfare was the reason for this period of decline.[63] It was during this time that Tikal was heavily focused on warfare. New technologies in warfare from Teotihuacán probably assisted in Tikal's military victories.[64] In contrast to the "star wars" of the past, this new kind of war, the "ax war" was symbolized by an ax glyph and indicated a serious war with intent to completely destroy.[65] In AD 679, Dos Pilas, a former ally, defeated Tikal, most likely with the assistance of Tikal's principal enemy, Calakmul. In describing the aftermath of this major battle, texts mention "pools of blood" and "piles of heads."[66]

We find it interesting that the final wars between the Nephites and Lamanites were taking place during this time. A bit more than two decades after Tikal's conquest of Uaxactún, Moroni describes the state of the land in Mormon 8:8, saying that after they had destroyed the Nephites, the Lamanites were fighting with each other and the entire land was the scene of continual murder and bloodshed, with no end to the war in sight.

## Prisons

The Central Acropolis grew and developed over the centuries, eventually turning into a maze of royal palaces, official buildings, residences, and courts, some isolated from each other. Most can be entered and explored, and carved wooden supports can still be seen spanning the corbelled ceilings. Near the southeast corner of this complex is a small open area called Court 4. Facing its west side is Structure 51. It is an unassuming, two-roomed structure that may have originally been living quarters. But certain details that turned up during its excavation have led Peter Harrison, an expert on Tikal, to speculate that it was used as a jail during the later periods of Tikal's history.[67] In addition to the unexpected combination of remnants of ancient food and human feces found here, unusual secondary holes in the doorjambs of this room may have been used as anchors for wooden bars, effectively locking people in. Who was detained here and under what circumstances have been lost to history.

Prisons are mentioned many times in the Book of Mormon. The first is in Mosiah 7:7 when Ammon and some of his group are jailed by King Limhi. The prophet Abinadi was cast into prison by the evil King Noah in Mosiah 14:8. Perhaps one of the most memorable events was when Alma and Amulek were imprisoned in Alma 14:17 and were later freed when the walls shook and fell to the ground. There are other examples, some dating back to the Jaredites. These accounts must have sounded anachronistic in Joseph Smith's day. Is it really plausible that jails existed in ancient America? What might they look like? Before Tikal, we could point to no such example, but here we have strong evidence that such things did happen. It is true that this jail at Tikal was used long after the end of the Book of Mormon, but now we know that people were imprisoned anciently, and we can surmise what a Lamanite prison would have looked like during Alma's time, since the building techniques have not changed much. If you can find Court 4, you can step into these small rooms and imagine what Alma would have felt, except that now the ceilings are mostly gone. We also found similar holes in other buildings bordering Court 4, so these may have been holding cells as well. The court is in quadrant 5D of the official site map. The best way to find it is to purchase a guidebook for Tikal and look in the section on the Central Acropolis for a detailed plan. If you do not already have one, they can be found for sale at Tikal's shops in a variety of languages.

*These holes look like good evidence for the existence of a jail cell. See how many you can find; be sure to check the buildings on both sides of Court 4.*

## Evidence of Metal Tools

Among the many artifacts with a high degree of artistry found at Tikal are the famous carved lintels from some of the major temples. These lintels are intricately carved with images and text, commemorating high points in kings' reigns that they wished to be remembered. Most have been removed from their original locations. Lintel 3 from Temple IV commemorates Yikin Chan Kawiil's victory over the site of El Perú and is currently on display in the national anthropological museum in Guatemala City. While most archaeologists still affirm that the Maya had no metal tools, they recognize that these lintels are carved from very hard sapodilla wood.[68] When John Stephens and Frederick Catherwood made their famous travels through Mesoamerica in the 19th

111

century, they discovered similar carved lintels at sites like Uxmal and Kabah. They realized that they were carved from a very hard wood and believed that metal tools must have been used to carve such fine details.[69] They also knew that the first European explorers did see examples of metal axes.

During excavations at Tikal, mirrors of pyrite and iron have been found.[70] The iron was not smelted, but most likely cold-hammered into shape. This is not metallurgy of the level mentioned in the Book of Mormon, but it does show that the inhabitants of Tikal recognized the value of this kind of material. Currently, evidence for metalworking as early as the Book of Mormon suggests has not been found in Mesoamerica, but metal implements from later periods are known and possible evidence of working with metal tools exists, even if the tools themselves are long gone. While it is still debatable how much and how early the Maya used metal tools, the archaeological record for earlier periods is incomplete and much may have been permanently lost.

## Tombs and Pyramids

This is not a similarity with the Book of Mormon per se, but it is worthy of mention. It is now well known that Tikal is rich with tombs and temple pyramids. Typical of Mayan burials was that the bones of the person buried were laid in a particular direction, often on a north/south axis, a sacred direction to the Maya, if the person was of some importance.[71] Usually offerings of jade, shell, ceramic vases, and other ceremonial items are found interred with the body. Sometimes certain body parts are removed or covered with items like jade masks. Jewelry was often placed in the hands, mouth, eyes, or other points on the body. Many details of Mesoamerican burials, such as sacrificing captives or servants and leaving food for the afterlife, are closely mirrored in the ancient burial practices of the Old World. However, mainstream acceptance of the idea that pyramids in Mesoamerica acted as tombs, in a similar fashion to those in ancient Egypt, is relatively new.

The city of Tikal was planned using triangulation and a right angle system.[72] Of this Peter Harrison remarks, "Observation of this remarkable feature of Tikal architecture raises more questions than it solves. Where did this knowledge come from? How, in practicality, was it executed over large distances on the surface and quite formidable ones in the vertical dimensions? Some answers may be derived from outside sources. The ancient Egyptians used the exact same system as a means of land measure to re-survey their fields after every annual flooding of the Nile. Later the system found its way into the design of their art and architecture. While there is no connection between the two societies, a similar process of development undoubtedly was in operation."[73]

According to most archaeologists, there are no cultural connections between Egypt and Mesoamerica. But the similarities in the use of pyramids, tombs, and city planning are striking. We know that Lehi, and even the Jews of his time, had strong ties to Egypt. We wonder if the learning of the Egyptians might have been passed on to the people of Mesoamerica and was possibly modified over time. We are not suggesting that all of these practices can be traced directly to groups mentioned in the Book of Mormon, but if in addition to Lehi's group, Mulekites and Jaredites crossed the ocean to arrive here, why not others? If the similarities that we mention are more than just coincidences, then there must have been some kind of contact between the Old and New Worlds anciently. Remember that a major objection to the Book of Mormon is that there is no evidence for this kind of contact so long ago. It just does not fit into the traditional view of the history of the Americas.

But the "Bering Strait Only" theory has its challengers. As time goes on, more mainstream scholars are coming to realize that this view is too restrictive. John Montgomery, an expert in pre-Columbian art and hieroglyphs, sees additional possibilities. Regarding the peopling of ancient America, he suggest, "Others perhaps crossed the Pacific Ocean from Asia in small vessels, and not inconceivably over the Arctic from Europe. Stylistic affinities with tools found in North America and Western Europe as far south as Spain suggest the peopling of the Americas may have been a much more complicated process than originally believed."[74] If this is true, then why not Lehi and the others mentioned in the Book of Mormon? These ancient voyages across the ocean seem more plausible today than when the Book of Mormon was first published.

# YAXHÁ

ongoing excavation work

the Mexican war god Tlaloc

small ballcourt

# How We Got There

Yaxhá is 90 kilometers from Flores and approximately 65 kilometers from Tikal. After spending most of the day at Tikal, we left in the afternoon taking CA 13 west toward the Belize border. As we got closer, the surroundings became more rural and the road, while still paved, gradually worsened. From time to time, we had to suddenly slow down or dodge large potholes that appeared at the last minute. We probably should have driven a bit more slowly and cautiously, but we were trying to reach Yaxhá before nightfall. From the main road, there is a turnoff to the left that is clearly marked, heading north to Yaxhá. After the turnoff, the pavement soon ended and we were on a dirt road, now made extremely muddy by all the recent rainfall.

About one and a half hours after leaving Tikal, we reached a small guard station three kilometers from the lake. We stopped at the barricade and were questioned regarding our stay and let in. The site closes at nightfall, and we had arrived just in time. There was no fee and we were directed to a camping area where we could set up our tents. The guards were very pleasant and suggested we have dinner at the El Sombrero hotel and restaurant a bit back down the road, even agreeing to let us back in afterward.

*(continued on page 118)*

116

## BACKGROUND

The average American will likely only know Yaxhá as the setting of the reality television show *Survivor* in 2005. Much of its history remains largely unknown. Of all the sites we visited, this one had the least amount of information. This is due to the fact that there are very few inscriptions at the site, and apparently very little archaeological work has been completed and published, although from what we could see, much excavation is currently underway. This is surprising for what was once such a large and important site.

The name Yaxhá means "blue green water" and is believed to be the original name of the site during the Classic period, something which is almost unheard of for Mayan sites.[1] The site has a long history, with occupation starting around 600 BC and lasting until AD 900.[2] Despite such a long period of occupation, we know almost nothing about its Preclassic history. The city of Yaxhá is quite large; it is the third largest ancient site in Guatemala, next to the ruins of Tikal and El Mirador. The city's core population is estimated by some experts to have peaked at 42,000 and was situated around *bajos*, or low wetlands.[3] Archaeologists believe these swampy areas provided ideal conditions for large-scale agriculture, allowing the Maya to sustain large populations in the surrounding areas.[4]

It appears that Yaxhá professed allegiance to nearby Tikal. They share some similar archaeological features, and Yaxhá is the only other site besides Tikal known to have a twin pyramid complex, built in commemoration of a *katun* or 20-year period.[5] The city also resembles the layouts of sites in the Yucatán like Cobá and Chichén Itzá, with roads connecting different areas and major groups of structures of the site. This stylistic influence from so far away is a bit surprising, but Stela 11 depicting a warrior goddess wearing a Tlaloc mask may show evidence of additional influence from the distant city of Teotihuacán.[6] So yet another Mayan site has had some form of interaction

## BOOK OF MORMON COMPARISONS

*Yaxhá was inhabited during Book of Mormon times, but sadly, next to nothing is known about its Preclassic history. It is also probably in the right area geographically, located in the northeastern edge of the lands mentioned in the scriptural record.*

# Right Time and Place

This site was inhabited since before Lehi's group landed and continued for centuries after the collapse of the Nephite nation. Since its historical record during this early period is probably lost forever, we may never know what happened at Yaxhá while Nephite and Lamanite history was transpiring. Although few lakeside cities are mentioned in the Book of Mormon, Yaxhá almost certainly was part of this region.

As with other Classic sites, most of the visible construction that remains today was built after most of the Book of Mormon events had taken place. But Structure 216, built on the highest point in Yaxhá, does date back to Preclassic times and was here by about AD 200.[17] It is possible that inhabitants here witnessed Book of Mormon events, but archaeology will probably not be able to answer that question for us.

The guards lifted up the gate and we drove in. By now, the dirt road was rutted, muddy, and slippery, so we were once again glad that we were driving in an SUV with four-wheel-drive capabilities. We would probably not have made it this far without them. Driving to the shores of Lake Yaxhá, not far from the entrance of the site, we were pleasantly surprised to see wooden platforms with thatched roofs that rose many feet off the ground. There was a firepit near picnic benches and tables, which for Guatemala was upscale. We unpacked our gear, and each climbed up his own personal camping platform to get ready for the night. We had spotted some large cockroaches on the floors, so we opted to sleep in our tents. As night fell, the views overlooking the lake below were spectacular. Signs near the shore of the lake warned of crocodiles in the water. Abundant wildlife could be heard all around. The thatched roofs, lake, and views made the whole place feel exotic (which it was). After preparing

(continued on page 120)

*Our camp on the shore of Lake Yaxhá*

with this enigmatic and powerful Mexican culture.

By the eighth century, Yaxhá had gained some independence, and new monuments were being erected. Stela 13 from this period records the name of king Kinich Lakamtun and two dates: AD 793 and 797.[7] Things seemed to be going well for this king and his city, but this prosperity was not to last. During the Classic period Yaxhá was often in conflict with the cities of Naranjo, some 20 kilometers to the northeast, and Calakmul. While not much has been found at Yaxhá itself, fortunately some surviving texts from Naranjo shed light on this struggle. Its Stelae 12 and 35 record an account of this war between Kinich Lakamtun and Itzamnaj Kawiil of Naranjo.[8] Stela 12 states that the conflict began in February of 799 and Stela 35 records Yaxhá's defeat in September of that same year. By May of AD 800, Kinich Lakamtun was paying tribute to Itzamnaj Kawill.[9] Eventually, after all these humiliations, the king of Yaxhá was captured and killed at Naranjo.

But that was not the end of Yaxhá's good fortune. By the middle of the ninth century, building activity resumed at the site. While populations were decreasing in this area of the Petén, the urban center at Yaxhá was experiencing a boom of sorts, with new palaces, monumental construction, and other renovations taking place. While no new monuments were carved at this time, many existing ones were moved to new locations.[10] For some unknown reason, while other sites in this region were collapsing at the end of the Classic period, Yaxhá was flourishing, its elite organizing the populations and overseeing ambitious building projects. There are even indications that after the demise of the mighty Tikal, its refugees fled here.[11] How Yaxhá's rulers were able to accomplish this feat remains a mystery.

Notwithstanding its ups and downs, Yaxhá's star eventually faded and it was abandoned, like all sites in the Petén. There was some Postclassic habitation here, probably by Maya from the Yucatán. Also, between AD 1100 and

## Ancient Name

A unique feature about Yaxhá is its name. It is well known that most archaeological sites do not currently have the names by which they were known in antiquity. Some, like El Mirador, Naranjo, Dos Pilas, Piedras Negras, and Palenque, have Spanish names that obviously are no older than the Conquest. Other names were known to the Maya and Aztecs but were usually given after the sites were abandoned. Still others, like Yaxchilán, Calakmul, and Becán, were named by archaeologists in modern times. In almost no cases do the names we know today match what the sites were called when they were inhabited.

Yaxhá is a rare exception. The lake near which it sits was already known as "Yaxhaa" in 1618 when Orbita and Fuensalida reached its shores.[18] The significance of this name was not known until 1975 when the site's glyph was identified. Epigraphic studies have shown that it can be transliterated as "yax-a," "yax-ah," or "yax-ha."[19] It is supposed that this was a name for both the lake and the city, dating back to the Classic period. This means that by the time the Spanish priests first heard the name, it was already about 1,200 years old, if not older.

Even though this name is quite old and probably dates to the end of Book of Mormon times, it is not known if this extends to the Preclassic era, when most of the Book of Mormon events took place. In fact, even though we now know the ancient names for many sites, none can be definitively dated

(continued on page 121)

for the night, we decided to take the advice of the guards and get some dinner.

We drove back up the road a ways and followed a sign that pointed to the El Sombrero Ecolodge. There was no artificial lighting this deep in the jungle, and we were surrounded by pitch blackness. To our dismay the place was completely dark and empty, but our hunger drove us to investigate. With our flashlights shining the way, we carefully picked our way through deep mud into the dense jungle night. Not long after getting out of our car, we came upon a walkway, and following it, were greeted by a young man who told us that they were indeed open, but needed to turn the generators on. That process must have taken a while, because he first brought out candles to our table. The place lit up and he showed us into the dining area. We sat down in a large open-air room that was more like a wooden deck with a roof over it. In a spacious sitting room, there were many books and items to look at as we waited for our food to be prepared. The same young man who showed us in took our orders and gave them to the cook in the back room. He was the only person that we saw at the place, but he was amiable and spoke to us while we waited and read books on local ecology and archaeology by candlelight. He was a student and was working at the lodge to earn money for school. Soon the generators kicked in and with better light, we were able to appreciate our setting a bit more.

*(continued on page 122)*

1450, people with ties to the Yucatán capital Mayapán were living on an island in the lake at a site called Topoxté,[12] but by the end of this period the sites were abandoned for good. In 1618, two Spanish friars, Orbita and Fuensalida, traveled through Belize and northern Guatemala, but although they came to Lake Yaxhá, they did not mention any indication of habitation in the region.[13]

As far as we know, Yaxhá's first non-native visitor was Teobert Maler in 1904, who made the first investigations of the site. It was later mapped by the Carnegie expedition in the 1930s. Isolated excavations began in the early 1970s under Nicholas Hellmuth.[14] Full-scale excavation and restoration did not begin until the late 1990s, and work continues in full force today. Major structures are still being renovated and the digs are ongoing, so there may be more to see and appreciate in the next few years.

## BRIEF SITE OVERVIEW

Not many people visit Yaxhá, and much of it is unrestored. The positive side to this is that we had the site all to ourselves. We did not see anyone else for the first couple of hours as we wandered around, and then it was only people working here, no other tourists. This site was the only one we visited in all of our travels where we actually witnessed people actively doing restoration or excavation work; we even saw bulldozers and other heavy machinery in use onsite.

Structure K is the first structure you come upon near the entrance. It is currently under restoration, which is being funded by Deutsche Bank. From there we walked to Structure 216, the largest structure at the site. This massive pyramid is about 100 feet high, with initial construction dating to the Preclassic period, and the final version being completed in AD 750.[15] We climbed up a series of wooden stairs to the top where we had read that we could see

(*Ancient Name continued*) past the Classic period because Mayan hieroglyphics are just not that old. Critics have pointed out that of the many place names in the Book of Mormon, none have been found through epigraphical studies. Looking at a map of Mesoamerica, we find no Zarahemla, Cumorah, or land of Nephi. The truth is that scholars really have no idea what these sites known today were called during the lifetimes of Mosiah, Alma, or Moroni. But the example of Yaxhá shows us that ancient names could actually refer to the sites themselves rather than the dynasties that ruled them.[20] Also significant is that a number of cities in the Book of Mormon had essentially the same ending as Yaxhá, such as Nephihah, Moronihah, and Onihah.

## Death by Fire

When Itzamnaj Kawiil of Naranjo finally killed Kinich Lakamtun of Yaxhá, he recorded his act on Stela 35. What is interesting is how the execution is depicted. Referring back to a mythical account of a young god killing a jaguar deity (a patron war god of Yaxhá) by fire, Itzamnaj Kawiil re-enacts that event by burning his captive. The stela shows him holding a large, flaming torch and standing over Kinich Lakamtun.[21] Why he chose this method of death instead of another is unknown.

The Book of Mormon records similar deaths. Because the prophet Abinadi would not recant his criticism of the wicked King Noah and his priests, he was put to death by fire in an unspecified manner in Mosiah 17:20. Later,
(continued on page 123)

After eating a very nice meal and leaving some extra money for our student friend, we drove back in the dark to our elevated tents. The El Sombrero lodge is a great (and the only) place to stay at Yaxhá. We recommend it if you are not fond of camping, although the amenities are limited to small thatched huts. Before turning in, we walked down to the shores of the lake, ever mindful of the crocodile warnings. All around us, fireflies flashed through the nighttime air. It was an incredible sight, and we tried unsuccessfully to take photos and video of them. Feeling quite exhausted by this point, we each climbed up the ladders to our tents and turned in for the night.

The sun was up by 6:00 a.m., and by 6:30 mosquitoes were already buzzing around our tents, drawn in by fresh blood. After spraying ourselves liberally with bug repellent, we packed up our gear and stowed it in the SUV. Since we were so near the site, we had planned on simply walking from our campground to it. However, as it was now beginning to rain, we decided to drive in to save some time and keep dry for a few minutes longer.

*Finally, we get to see some actual excavation work.*

122

awe-inspiring views of the lake and surrounding jungle. Unfortunately for us, the weather was so overcast and foggy that we could hardly see beyond the structure's base. We did notice a circular stone-ringed pit on the ground that reminded us of the areas at Tikal and other sites still used by the Maya for religious ceremonies.

We walked down the stairs and headed toward Plaza A, situated on an artificially elevated platform. It is here that we found the twin-pyramid complex, similar to the seven such complexes at Tikal. While similarities undoubtedly exist, there are some differences as well. Yaxhá's complex does not have stelae and monuments placed as its Tikal examples do. Also, the building on the northern edge does not match the nine-doored palaces seen at Tikal.[16] Why these structures are so similar and yet different is not known. Currently, the pyramids are not much to look at since they remain unrestored.

From here we made our way to the North Acropolis, which was recently restored and is one of the more interesting groups of buildings at the site. Excavation work was in full force here with workers and equipment running continually while we climbed around. We climbed to the top of the northernmost structure at the Acropolis. From here, the views at the top were spectacular so that we could see the surrounding site as the fog lifted, getting a better perspective on the layout of the area.

From the North Acropolis we walked a while on a muddy road northward to what is called the Palace and the Maler Group. Here you can see a few stelae, but most are worn and not particularly interesting. Although the site as a whole has relatively few stelae, we did enjoy

Stela 11 with its depiction of the Tlaloc mask of the Mexican war god. Groups in this area, like the Maler Group and the North and East Acropolises, were part of Yaxhá's later building and renovation efforts. The stelae in these areas were likely moved from their original locations at that time. From here we began walking southward back toward the entrance.

On our way back we passed the east side of the North Acropolis and found workers busy in a roped-off area, excavating the side of a structure. They were digging through outer walls into a temple's side, exposing a previous layer that had a large mask attached to the side of the building. This is a common feature of ancient structures, as the Maya built over existing structures, enlarging them to make them more sacred with every new layer of construction. The workers let us take a look at it and talked to us a bit about what they were doing but would not allow us to take close-up photographs of the excavation and were especially strict about it. We could find no one who appeared to be in charge of the whole operation. Usually, archaeologists oversee these digs. The workers were nice enough, but we had hoped they would have been a bit more accommodating.

We continued on. Along the way we saw a ballcourt, which was probably the smallest we had seen so far. Workers there were restoring what looked like a palace or residential structure at its far end. We took a moment to climb up and converse with them about what they were doing. After seeing them mix mortar and fit stones back together, we realized that much of the appearance of these sites is due to the modern restoration work that literally rebuilds these crumbled ruins. We continued on our way out to the entrance, taking one last look at the serene lake and peaceful surroundings. Overall, Yaxhá is a site that we would recommend seeing, but for different reasons than most other sites. Its appeal comes from its lack of commercialization and extensive restoration of most areas, very few visitors, and its gorgeous lakeside setting.

*(Death by Fire continued)* when Noah's people rebel against him for his less than honorable ways, they do the same to him in Mosiah 19:20. In Alma chapter 14, people who believed Alma's and Amulek's teachings were cast into a fire, along with their scriptures, to be burned. Of course, these accounts mentioned in the scriptures occurred centuries before Kinich Lakamtun's death, but the image on the stela at Naranjo is proof that such things did happen. Perhaps because of the connection with the death of a god in Mayan myth, execution by fire had an additional ritual significance.

## Agricultural Support for Large Populations

The traditional view has been that the Maya practiced an agricultural technique known as "slash-and-burn." This may certainly be the case in some areas, but it does not produce enough crops to sustain a high population density, such as the more than 250 people per square mile in nearby Tikal.[22] The Maya must have developed more sophisticated agricultural methods to feed the masses of people living in large centers like Tikal and other large sites in the Petén. The same can be said of other areas with large cities like Calakmul, Tikal's rival in more than just size. Yaxhá seems to have functioned as a "breadbasket" of sorts for the populations in the surrounding region. The fertile soil of the *bajos* surrounding Yaxhá, coupled with advanced farming methods like terracing and irrigation canals, provided enough food for the hundreds of thousands (if not more) living in just the Petén.

The Book of Mormon mentions very large populations at some periods. According to Ether 15:2, millions were killed during the last Jaredite battles. In the final battle between the Nephites and Lamanites, Mormon chapter 6 records that the Nephite armies were apparently divided into 21 units of 10,000 each, and they faced an even larger army. Even if these numbers were exaggerated, as is often the case in ancient documents, such a battle implied extremely large population bases. Agriculture is only referred to in general terms in the Book of Mormon. Corn is mentioned as the dominant crop, but no further details are discussed. These numbers may seem extravagant and would be impossible to support using simple farming techniques, but now we know that the Maya were quite advanced in agriculture and could provide enough food to support such numbers, at least until the collapse at the end of the Classic period.

# QUIRIGUÁ

Zoomorph G

"full-figure" hieroglyph

plaza and acropolis

# QUIRIGUÁ

## How We Got There

We learned from our 15-hour drive from Panajachel to not underestimate driving time and to appreciate the value of staying on the main highways in Guatemala. We had planned to drive to Quiriguá from Yaxhá, tour the site, and then drive to Copán in Honduras before the border closed, all in one day. With this in mind, we made sure to take a quick tour of Yaxhá that morning and were on the road by 9:30 a.m. The drive from Yaxhá to Quiriguá covered 550 kilometers and luckily ended up only taking about three and a half hours. This time, our return from the lowlands back to the highlands of Guatemala was much more enjoyable than our earlier trek up to Bethel from the other side of the country. These roads were quite good, and besides being stuck behind an occasional convoy of freight trucks, we were able to move along at a relatively fast pace. Leaving the jungle lowlands of the Petén, the roads got increasingly curvy as we went through the mountains.

We continued traveling for some time on CA 13, which at one point runs almost to the border of Belize. In this region the scenery took on a more Caribbean look and feel. Of particular interest was crossing a bridge over Lake Izabal, a massive freshwater lake that eventually empties into

(continued on page 128)

126

## BACKGROUND

Quiriguá appears to be a smaller city in comparison to other Mayan sites, but its true size is unknown. Its urban population never went over a few thousand during its history.[1] Yet this site contains some of the greatest stelae and carvings in the Mayan world. It is located between important resources of jadeite and obsidian and was built alongside the Motagua River, which has changed course since the Classic period; the riverbed is now about one kilometer south of the site.[2] For 300 years, trade connections of these precious commodities were controlled by Copán through Quiriguá, its subordinate. Tikal most likely ruled over both Copán and Quiriguá during this early history, which gave Tikal access to important trade routes and resources.[3]

The city of Quiriguá was founded in AD 426 by Tok Casper, whose inauguration was done under the authority of Yax Kuk Mo, king of Copán at the time.[4]

Monument 26, discovered accidentally in 1978 by a Guatemalan subsidiary of Del Monte, has a date that is most likely AD 493, the earliest known outside of the site's core.[5] Not much is known about the history of Quiriguá for the next 300 years, but we do know that at some point during the sixth or early seventh century, a major flood caused by some natural disaster buried the whole city beneath a deep layer of silt. Only Group A and portions of 3C-1, built on the highest points of elevation, remained above ground after the disaster.[6]

In AD 724 Cauac Sky (also known as Kak Tiliw Chan Yoaat) was made king. Typical of all the previous rulers at Quiriguá, the ceremony took place under the supervision of a Copán king. Like his predecessors, Cauac Sky was a sub-king, owing his authority and allegiance to Copán, now ruled by a king named 18-Rabbit. But this kind of supervision would end under Cauac Sky's reign. In an unexpected twist of history, he rebelled against the much larger Copán and became the most influential ruler that Quiriguá would ever know.[7]

## BOOK OF MORMON COMPARISONS

*Compared to other sites, Quiriguá's history is relatively brief and known archaeological remains date only to the Classic period after the close of Book of Mormon history. The site is small and surviving structures are few, but there are a few interesting traces here.*

### Buried City

Many natural disasters have occurred throughout the history of Mesoamerica and civilizations have rebuilt and kept going. Between the sixth and early seventh centuries AD, a massive flood hit this valley and buried the site under many layers of silt and alluvial deposits. What the circumstances were surrounding this event are unknown; possible causes for this disaster are an erupting volcano or a strong hurricane. Only the settlements on higher ground, such as the early Group A to the north, remained untouched. Much of Quiriguá is still buried and the true extent of its size is only guessed at. Most of what is now visible was built afterward.

The cataclysmic events at the time of the Savior's death resulted in the destruction of many cities. In 3 Nephi 9:8, the Lord himself speaks to the people and specifically names Gadiandi, Gadiomnah, Jacob, and Gimgimno as having been sunk, or buried under the earth, so that hills and valleys were now in their place. This was done to hide their wickedness. The flooding and burial of Quiriguá happened centuries after this event, but now we know that such things did indeed happen.

the Gulf of Honduras. We wished we could have spent some time there as it was very beautiful and scenic. We had read that manatee and other exotic wildlife live in the area.

The passing lanes are one thing to watch out for. Usually, the road had just two lanes, one for each direction. But at times, the road would open up and we would have an extra passing lane on our side, while the other direction would only have a single lane. These passing lanes would sometimes wind around curves. We almost experienced a head-on collision more than once when using these passing lanes because drivers coming from the opposite direction would cross over and use our passing lane, even around blind curves. We learned to treat passing lanes as serving both sides of the road at the same time, despite the solid double line separating the opposing traffic from our lanes.

CA 13 runs into CA 9, where we turned right and headed southwest until we reached a turnoff to the ruins, which were four kilometers down a small road from the pavement. This bumpy road to the ruins is lined on either side with the banana trees of what used to be the Del Monte plantation. At the end, we turned right into the parking lot for Quiriguá. It is small, but when we were there the site was not crowded, so we had no problem finding a space.

In 738 Cauac Sky somehow seized 18-Rabbit, the same very king that had overseen his rise to kingship, and decapitated him. It appears that a conspiracy to seize the king may have come into play here. In the surviving texts, no recognizable term for war between the two sites has been found during this time.[8] How could such a smaller, subordinate site have achieved a major coup against a powerful entity like Copán? Texts have been deciphered showing that a mere two years after his accession to the throne, Cauac Sky hosted a king from Calakmul at an important ceremony at Quiriguá. This king may have been Wamaw Kawill, successor to Yuknoom Took, who may have been defeated and captured by a king of Tikal.[9] This event indicates a possible link to Tikal's chief rival, and therefore, a likely enemy of Copán. The relationship that developed may have been the start of a possible change in allegiance that could have given Quiriguá enough military power to deliver such a crushing blow against Copán, an ally of Tikal.[10]

Released from the bonds of servitude to Copán and with a new commanding influence over the Motagua trade route, Quiriguá thrived economically. After 18-Rabbit's demise, Quiriguá's emblem glyph was used for the first time. The surrounding valley was used for cacao cultivation, which may be why the emblem glyph appears to show a cacao tree. Many structures were built and remodeled and the tallest stelae in the Mayan world were dedicated during this time.[11] Much of what we see at the site today was built during this period of prosperity brought on by Cauac Sky's daring victory. Perhaps to support these building projects, populations in Quiriguá and the surrounding areas grew dramatically.[12] After an unusually long 60 years of ruling, Cauac Sky finally died in AD 785.[13] Not long afterward, Quiriguá began to slide into decline.

The last known king was Jade Sky, who came into power starting between 795 and 800. He rebuilt the Acropolis and erected two small monuments. He even celebrated a *katun* ending with Yax Pasah, the 16th king of Copán. This surprising event may have signaled a return to peaceful relations between the two sites.[14] Not much more is known about his reign, but the last date found at the site is AD 810. Within a few years, the site was abandoned.[15] Similar to Yaxhá, Quiriguá appears to have been re-inhabited for a while during a later period, perhaps by settlers from as far away as Chichén Itzá.[16]

Stephens and Catherwood were the first to bring Quiriguá to the attention of the outside world in the 19th century with the publication of their book *Incidents of Travel in Central America, Chiapas, and Yucatan*. Even though it was one of the first sites they visited and it contains the largest and finest examples of Mayan sculptured monuments, Frederick Catherwood only produced a couple of drawings of Quiriguá's stelae, and they are not even particularly detailed. This may have been because they were so overgrown by the time they arrived. It was also the first site visited by the great Mayanist Alfred Maudslay, who spent several months there, photographing monuments. Excavations in the early 20th century were directed by Edgar Lee Hewett and Sylvanus Morley. From 1974 to 1979 the University of Pennsylvania worked with Guatemala's archaeological institute to conduct major projects and renovations at the site,[17] finally drawing much-deserved attention to Quiriguá.

## False Beards

From time to time, we see examples of bearded figures in Mayan art. Some of the representations are of natural facial hair, but many of the stelae at Quiriguá depict what are obviously false beards on the king. Similar examples can be seen at nearby Copán. This stylistic similarity attests to the socio-political connection between the two sites.

While explicitly disavowing any cultural ties with ancient Egypt, John Stephens did compare the stelae at Copán to Egyptian art when describing the beards. We include this reference here because this feature is even more striking in the stelae at Quiriguá and some are amazingly Egyptian-looking. Stelae A, C, D, E, and F have long, narrow beards on the chins of otherwise beardless faces. Why the king had himself depicted this way is still a mystery, but then, we are not entirely sure why the Egyptians did it, either. Since the stelae show the king with symbols of divine power and authority, could the beards have been one of these symbols? We are not claiming a direct link between the Classic Maya and ancient Egypt, but perhaps there were legends or cultural memories of powerful bearded figures from their past. If so, who were these bearded people?

# BRIEF SITE OVERVIEW

The true extent of Quiriguá's actual size may never be known because all but the highest points have been buried. Many important finds away from the central core have been made by accident by workers on the surrounding banana plantation digging irrigation canals.[18] The portion of the site that is open to visitors is relatively small and only requires a few hours to see. It is well worth the visit though, since it contains the largest and some of the greatest carvings in the Mayan world. It is also known for its zoomorphs, which are intricately carved boulders that take the form of various animals, intertwined with hieroglyphic writing and rulers' portraits. The site has only a few structures and is mostly flat, grassy pasture with various stelae and zoomorphs dotting the area, but other known structures exist to the north and west. You enter the site at the northern end of the Great Plaza and walk on a path into an open area surrounded by dense forest. Just past the entrance to the left is Structure 1A-3, a minor structure that is unrestored and so eroded and covered with vegetation that we did not recognize it as anything other than a long hill. It frames the northern edge of the Great Plaza.

From here, the site opens up and is mainly a setting for the many stelae and two zoomorphs, B and G. All but two of the stelae (the smallest ones) were erected by Cauac Sky in the mid-eighth century AD. His portrait appears on A, C, D, E, F, H, and J. Stelae A, C, and D are lined up in front of Structure 1A-3. Most of the monuments are of a very fine-grained sandstone and are in an excellent state of preservation. Many of the original carved details can still be seen. The texts on Stela C recount the creation date of this present cycle in 3114 BC. It describes that placement of three cosmic stones that framed the first act of creation.[19] In front of these three stelae is the large, squat Zoomorph B, carved into a cosmic crocodile covered with glyphs from a boulder weighing several tons.

After viewing this first group, we continued across a brief open space to see Stelae E and F. Several of the tallest stelae in the Mayan world are found here, and Stela E has the honor of being the largest. Weighing in at 30 tons and rising to a height of 24 feet (with even more below ground), it is truly massive. Just past them, Zoomorph G describes Cauac Sky's death and burial. Three zoomorphs (G, O, and P) were commissioned by Sky Xul, Cauac Sky's successor, during his relatively short reign. Although few in number, they are simply astounding in their size and complexity. There are not many buildings here, but the Great Plaza has the most extensive setting for royal monuments in the Mayan area. At 1,066 feet long, it is larger than any other. It has been suggested that the layout of the stelae, the Great Plaza, and the Acropolis to the south was to mimic or even surpass the design of Copán's ceremonial center after the death of 18-Rabbit. But further investigation into stylistic similarities may indicate that Quiriguá owes more of its design and fortune to Tikal rather than to its rival Copán.[20]

We continued our way through the Great Plaza, walking over thick grass that had suddenly become wet and marshy. Observing the great monuments along the way, we noticed Stela K, a portrait of Jade Sky, the last king. By contrast, this monument is quite small and diminutive, perhaps an

## "And It Came to Pass"

The more we studied texts at the various sites, the more examples of these glyphs we found, and Quiriguá is no exception. For the greatest number of them in one spot, look on the west side of Stela E. The glyphs are in two columns, labeled left to right A and B by archaeologists, who then number the rows from top to bottom. Using this nomenclature, glyphs reading *i-u-ti* can be found in blocks A6, A12, A14, and B16. They can all be translated as "and then it came to pass."

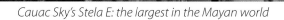

*Cauac Sky's Stela E: the largest in the Mayan world*

indication of dwindling resources near Quiriguá's end. Looking back, we wonder if Jade Sky would have had a bit of stela envy. Just past his unfortunate monument, we finally reached the Acropolis, a group of residential and administrative buildings surrounding several courts. Within one court are Zoomorphs P and O. P recounts the founding of Quirigua by Tok Casper and is considered one of the greatest carvings in the Mayan world. The court's east side was reserved as an ancestral shrine and was one of the earliest constructions at the Acropolis. A crypt was found here with the bones of an adult male that some archaeologists believe are the remains of the founder, Tok Casper.[21] To the south, Structure 1B-1 has the last date of AD 810 at the site.

To the east of the Acropolis is, not surprisingly, the East Group, a small collection of structures. South of the Acropolis is, you guessed it, the South Group. They are not much to see compared to the monuments and Acropolis. Honestly, about the only real reason to come here is the stelae, but that is reason enough; they are worth the trip. On our way out, we stopped to take a look at the small museum near the entrance. It has examples of early carving and artifacts at the site but mostly appears to be dedicated to jade artifacts. We then spent some time at the vendors surrounding the parking lot, browsing their selection to find some souvenirs to bring back home. We found out that buying a few small items may prompt some vendors to dig in their claws to get as much as they can out of you, as an old woman followed us out to our car, still trying to get us to buy T-shirts while we drove away as politely as we could.

These glyphs can also be found on Stela C. On the west side are two columns of text. Not counting the large, initial series glyph at the top that spans both columns, two examples of *i-u-ti* can be seen in B3 and B9, while an *utiya* can be seen in A7, using the same labeling system as on Stela E. *Utiya* can be translated as "it had come to pass."

The writing is amazingly well preserved, perhaps because of the quality of the sandstone. They are beautifully carved and many fine details are still visible. Take a look at the other stelae at the site to see if you can fine any more examples of this glyphic phrase.

Obviously, these phrases were written centuries after the close of the Book of Mormon and in a completely different writing system. There may be no direct connection, but we find it quite interesting that this phrase is so common in Mayan writing. Before these glyphs were translated, it could have been argued that Joseph Smith merely took this phrase from the Bible as a way to fill space in the text, but its usage in actual Mesoamerican writing weakens that argument considerably.

## The Tree of Life

The sacred tree of life, sometimes known as the Mayan cross or *axis mundi*, was one of the most important symbols in the Mayan religion. We include this topic at so many sites because depictions in one form or another of this tree are so widespread. Mayan kings used it as a symbol of their own divine right to rule, a connection with the world beyond, and their own resurrection and pathway to the heavens. In Quiriguá, a slightly different application of these concepts can be seen embodied in Stela F. Here, the king actually becomes the sacred tree of life, with the double-headed serpent in his hands and the celestial bird Itzam-Ye on his head.[26] Not merely is the tree his connection to the divine, but he has now become divine by portraying himself thus. He is, for all intents and purposes, the god of his people.

In the chapter on Palenque, we point out some similarities in Mayan belief about their tree of life and doctrines taught in the Book of Mormon. Since both the tree in the Garden of Eden and the tree in Lehi's dream represent eternal life and the greatest gift of God, we suggest that it can serve as a symbol for the atonement. The climax of his atoning sacrifice occurred when Jesus Christ was lifted up and crucified on a cross, or tree. These teachings may have been passed on through cultural diffusion and gradually evolved into the beliefs and reverence the Maya still have for the sacred cross/tree. The true significance has obviously been lost, but traces of true doctrine still may shine through.

## Divinity of Kings and Sacrifice

While shocking and reprehensible to the Spanish who first witnessed it, human sacrifice was seen as a necessary form of worship among the Maya and other people of Mesoamerica. The cosmos required the shedding of blood to maintain life, and this was the most sacred gift the Maya could give to the gods.[27] For this reason, and also to communicate with the spiritual realm, kings, queens, and other nobles practiced ritualistic bloodletting upon themselves, piercing parts of their bodies to be able to offer this precious substance. But the gods and the cosmos would not be satisfied with the few drops obtained by such acts; they also required the lives of sacrificial victims.

That the upstart Cauac Sky was able to capture and sacrifice the unfortunate 18-Rabbit from Copán was surprising, but only because Quiriguá was a small, subordinate site. The Maya engaged in capturing and sacrificing victims for centuries. It appears that nobles (*ahauob*) and especially kings were the preferred sacrifices.[28] If the kings were considered gods, then this would make sense. What better gift to offer the gods than the divine blood of another god? The sacrificial victim was re-enacting the death of the maize god in the underworld of Xibalba anyway,[29] so this is another indication of the divine personified in human sacrifice. Perhaps if Mayan kings saw themselves as gods, they viewed other kings, even rival ones, as gods as well.

We wonder if these beliefs and practices might have an element of truth at their source. Book of Mormon prophets were explicit in teaching that the very God of heaven would come to earth as a man to offer himself as a perfect and final sacrifice to atone for mankind's sins by shedding his own blood. Perhaps through centuries of apostasy, these teachings became the justification for human sacrifice, especially if the victims were considered to be gods. The concept of kingship is an ancient one in Mesoamerica. Kings are mentioned among both Lamanites and Nephites in the Book of Mormon; there were righteous and evil ones among both groups. That these kings considered themselves divine is not mentioned in the record, but since known Mesoamerican cultures had this practice, the righteous Nephite king Benjamin may have been aware of it as well. Perhaps this is why in Mosiah 2:10–11 King Benjamin told his people, "I have not commanded you to come up hither that ye should fear me, or that ye should think that I of myself am more than a mortal man. But I am like as yourselves, subject to all manner of infirmities in body and mind."

# Right Place

Quiriguá lies in what was probably the Land Southward spoken of in the Book of Mormon. Interestingly enough, it is also near the southeastern edge of the Mayan region. Along with Copán, it represents the southern extent of major cities in the Mayan culture. It was also one of the first ruined cities Stephens and Catherwood visited and is mentioned in their first published work, *Incidents of Travel in Central America, Chiapas, and Yucatan*.

This book caused quite a stir of interest among the general public and especially leaders of the Church at that time. Until that point, there had been no indication of the high levels of ancient civilization mentioned in the Book of Mormon. Regardless of longstanding beliefs that the Land Northward may have been North America and that the last battle took place in New York, the editors of *The Times and Seasons* (including Joseph Smith) published excerpts from Stephens and Catherwood's book, equating the cities they found with those mentioned in the Book of Mormon, even going so far as to suggest that Quiriguá might actually be Zarahemla, although they did not positively declare that.[30]

These articles demonstrate at least some rudimentary understanding that Book of Mormon events took place in Mesoamerica, at least after *Incidents* was published. With this geographical model in mind, Quiriguá definitely fits. However, based on an internal map of Book of Mormon geography, it probably cannot be Zarahemla, which was north of the land of Nephi and near the north-flowing River Sidon. Also, unknown to Stephens and Catherwood was the time period of the ruins they found, so it was easy to equate them to cities like Zarahemla and Bountiful. But now we know that Quiriguá's history begins around the close of the scriptural record, so the visible remains are not old enough. Evidence of settlement before AD 400 in the Motagua River Valley is rare, but these remains are buried over six feet below the present ground level,[31] so it is next to impossible to fully understand Quiriguá's early history. The site that can be seen and visited today is not a Book of Mormon city, but may have been built on or near settlements dating back to Nephite times.

# GETTING THERE: HONDURAS

From what we saw of Honduras, it is a beautiful country. We did not see much of it, as we went there for one reason: Copán. The amazing ruins of Copán are conveniently located within five hours of Guatemala City. The route is easy to follow and well worth the journey. Coming from the Petén in the north, we arrived from the opposite direction, but the same applies. Leaving Quiriguá at 2:00 in the afternoon, we arrived at the border less than three hours later. The scenery was beautiful as we traveled through different geological zones. The foliage changed from lush and green in the Motagua River Valley around Quiriguá to dry and arid as we approached the border.

The only major paved road on this side of Guatemala is CA 9. Although it is small with just one lane for each direction of traffic, it is in good repair and pleasant to drive on. Our only hindrance was that we got stuck behind many large trucks that impeded our progress until we found a way around them. On the sometimes steep and curvy mountainous road, this can require a heavy foot and nerves of steel. We were also stopped from time to time for construction or some other reason, but these delays were not long and nothing like what we had experienced during our drive north on the other side of the country.

On one occasion making our way though the hills and towns, we got behind a large tour bus before reaching the border. We were not able to pass for a while, but as we got closer, it looked as if something was thrown out of the bus. Not much later, we saw it again and realized that its passengers were throwing things out of the windows on purpose. The funny thing was that as we continued watching, we realized they were throwing things directly at pedestrians they passed along the way. Our initial surprise gave way to continual amusement as we continued to watch and count how many times the bus occupants did this. They must not have been worried about prosecution from strict littering laws. Finally, after watching someone almost crash his bike after being hit with multiple objects from the bus, curiosity got the best of us and we stopped to look for what they were throwing. What could be the reason for such bizarre behavior? Did the bus riders have an important message or warning to share? Were they mad at the local inhabitants? Or did they just not have a garbage can onboard and did not mind trashing Guatemala? When we found and picked up what they had been throwing out, we learned of another way others have to share the Gospel: write a scripture and proselytizing message on a small piece of paper, tie it around a small rock, and throw it at people as you drive by in a bus. It was amusing to watch and must be much easier than knocking on doors. But we do not know if their message was appreciated by those receiving it.

Crossing the border was easier than expected. All day we had been pushing to arrive at the Honduran border since the guidebooks had mentioned that it closed each evening. We could not remember if this was at 5:00 or 6:00, but supposedly, after it closes no vehicles can be driven across until morning, although foot traffic is still allowed. Needing to reach the town of Copán

Ruinas this evening and having no other place to stay, we did not want to arrive too late.

Shortly before 5:00 in the afternoon, we arrived at the border zone. The way into Honduras was blocked with a barrier, but we were on time and the place was still alive with activity. We did not see any signs or other indication that the border actually closed down each night, so we still are not sure about that one. In front of the gate were several small buildings along the left side of the road. Here we got out of our vehicle and were directed from window to window to pay a fee and receive stamps in our passports that allowed entrance to Honduras. Most guidebooks mention that travelers are not legally required to pay a fee. This was not the case with us and seeing the fee was minimal, we did not see it worth arguing the matter. Sometimes refusing the custom in favor of the letter of the law can cause more problems than it solves. We were surprised they did not ask for any documentation for our car. At the rental office near the airport in Guatemala City, the agency required us to pay extra for a document allowing us to take our car into Honduras. We were told that without this form, we would not be allowed to enter. For us this was not the case and we were allowed to cross over without showing the documentation, although it probably would not be wise to take the chance. If we had been asked for these papers in Honduras and been unable to produce them, the fine would have been extremely steep.

As with the other border, there were various people hanging around on the streets, offering to exchange money into lempiras, the Honduran currency. They did not appear to be officials, just locals walking around with large wads of cash in their pockets. This may seem a little questionable, but they gave us a decent exchange rate. With a little effort, you can sometimes get a better rate than what is originally offered. As with many goods and services, haggling is an acceptable way to do business.

With our passports stamped and money changed, the gate was lifted and we drove into Honduras, excited to be entering the third country on this little expedition. We followed the road that took us straight into the town of Copán Ruinas, where our next objective was to find a place to stay for the night.

*Macaws are a common sight in Copán.*

137

# COPÁN

legged serpent altar

macaw ballcourt marker

the "Five Katun" lord

## How We Got There

Anciently, there probably was a direct route for the 50-kilometer distance between Quiriguá and Copán, but in modern times the road is much more circuitous, going around small mountain ranges and through several towns. There is also the added hassle of passing from one country to another: dealing with passports, entry fees, and money exchanges. We had arrived in time to cross the border before it closed for the evening, and we continued the short drive into the town next to the site. The ruins of Copán are located 1.5 kilometers outside a modern town called, oddly enough, Copán Ruinas.

Getting to the town center was a little difficult as the road we were on eventually turned into a narrow, twisty dirt road winding through a little neighborhood of houses. We followed it, heading generally in the direction of what we believed was the central plaza. We were actually on the right track but ended up going the wrong way down a one-way street. A policeman loudly brought this to our attention, but when we stopped to talk to him and explain where we were trying to go, he was very helpful and pointed us in the right direction.

One block away from the center of town, the Parque Central, we found an empty space along

(continued on page 142)

## BACKGROUND

The fertile Copán Valley was inhabited by at least 900 BC.[1] Stela 17 (smashed and broken long ago) and other monuments record a date of AD 159, which may be the establishment of the kingdom.[2] But the history of the site really begins in AD 426 with the arrival of Yax Kuk Mo (First Quetzal-Macaw), considered the first king of Copán and the founder of a dynasty that would last for four centuries.[3] The events surrounding his rise to power are unclear, but we do know some interesting facts about Yax Kuk Mo. Studies of strontium isotopes in his teeth reveal that he spent his childhood in Tikal. His skeleton had many healed fractures, so he may have been a mighty warrior. Perhaps he took Copán by force.[4]

What brought him to the very outskirts of the Mayan region and how did he establish such an influential ruling dynasty here? These questions have not been fully answered. Before his arrival, ceramics in the area were characteristic of the Lenca, a local non-Mayan people. Yax Kuk Mo was definitely an outsider to this region, from a different cultural group

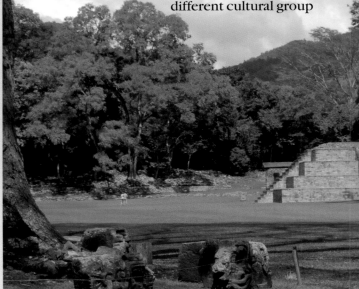

altogether. During his reign, ceramics appeared at Copán in the style of Teotihuacán.[5] This imported style continued for much of Copán's history, showing strong economic ties not only to that central Mexican city, but to Kaminaljuyú as well, indicating that although Yax Kuk Mo's kingdom was on the far reaches of the Mayan region, it was by no means isolated from the rest of the Classic city-states.[6] Copán's emblem glyph is a bat head and its ancient name was Xukpi, combining the Mayan words for "corner" and "sacred bundle."[7] This name seems to reflect its location at the far southeastern corner of the area populated by the Maya.

Yax Kuk Mo used imagery from Teotihuacán to declare his own connection to the Ah Puh, an almost mythical people believed by the Maya to have invented civilization, the arts, writing, and war.[8] These people have been identified as the Toltecs, coming from the legendary city of Tollan. Their culture is found at many sites, even at sites as far north as Chichén Itzá.

## BOOK OF MORMON COMPARISONS

*We doubt that Copán fits directly into Book of Mormon history, most likely being located too far south. People have certainly lived in this region for a long time, but its recorded history began shortly after Mormon finished the plates. However, a closer examination of Copán can give us a greater understanding of what really happened in Mesoamerica.*

### False Beards

Some of the stelae representing 18-Rabbit have beards and some do not. Why this is, we do not know. It is almost certain that he did not have a beard, as facial hair among the native races in these areas is not common. Depictions of beards are rare and archaeologists concede that the beards at Copán are probably false, although why the king would want himself depicted this way and what they might mean are unclear.[52] It is obvious that the Maya knew about people that had beards; some carvings and paintings of bearded figures from ancient Mesoamerica are genuine. But if the beardless king 18-Rabbit had portraits of himself made with beards, they must have symbolized something that had importance to him. Since the stelae at Copán are replete with imagery of divine authority and right to rule, we suggest that the beards could have symbolized this as well.

the street and parked at the curb. After our negative experience in Antigua Guatemala, we were very careful to look around for signs or other indications that we would not be parking illegally. Then we took a stroll through the town to find a hotel for the night. Amenities like hotels, restaurants, and shops are centered around the main plaza. Our first goal was to find a place to stay for the night, and we eventually decided on the Plaza Copán hotel just across the street on the eastern side of the Parque Central. This was a large, very nice hotel with an English-speaking receptionist and, most important, they accepted credit cards. After unloading luggage in the small and very cramped space in front of the hotel, we were directed down the street a few blocks to the locked and guarded parking lot for guests. We were pleased with a secure place to keep our rental car and there really was nowhere else to park.

Later we split up to take in various activities. One of us decided on a massage arranged by the hotel and was picked up and taken to the massage parlor on a tuk-tuk, a kind of three-wheeled motorbike/taxi. These little vehicles are a common way of getting around here, but they are so underpowered that they cannot make it up the steep hills of the town's streets, needing instead to go back and forth at an angle to the hill, crisscrossing their way up. It was later reported to the other two that the massage was not that great, plus the hotel key somehow bounced out of his pocket either coming or going, so we are not sure that this was such a good idea after all.

142    (continued on page 144)

Yax Kuk Mo had a large number of structures built very quickly and construction continued throughout the reigns of successive kings. Although Copán had some form of ties to major centers like Tikal and Palenque, it appears never to have been subordinate to any other site.[9] From very early times, it had connections with the nearby site of Quiriguá and controlled the traffic of valuable resources like jade and obsidian.[10] The 12th king of Copán, Smoke Jaguar, had a very long reign and dominated Quiriguá for 67 years.[11] However, Copán's good fortune would come to an unexpected end during the reign of his son.

The 13th king of Copán was named Waxaklahun-Ubah-Kawil. For simplicity's sake, we will refer to him by the translation of his name, 18-Rabbit. He is perhaps the most famous of Copán's kings and most of the stelae in the Great Plaza were commissioned by him to represent his divine power and authority. He took the throne in AD 695 and removed or defaced many of the monuments of previous kings.[12] Some of the greatest artistic achievements in the Mayan world were completed during his reign, but he is perhaps most famous for the sudden and dramatic way his life ended. In AD 738, Cauac Sky (or Kak Tiliw), the king of Quiriguá, captured and killed 18-Rabbit, probably by beheading him. It is not known how such a small subordinate site could triumph over a more powerful one like Copán. Adding to the mystery is the fact that there is no evidence of warfare, siege, or the accession of an outside ruler after 18-Rabbit's death.[13] A tantalizing piece of evidence is found in texts that mention the king of Calakmul at a period-ending celebration at Quiriguá during the previous year.[14] Since practically all southern lowland

Classic sites had an alliance with either Tikal or Calakmul,[15] the great warring superpowers of the era, Cauac Sky of Quiriguá may have had military help from Calakmul. Copán's ties to Tikal and its ally Palenque are already known.

While this defeat marked a decline in monumental construction at Copán,[16] a 14th king took power not long after 18-Rabbit's death and apparently showed his defiance of Quiriguá by keeping the Great Plaza as a memorial to the former king. In fact, Cauac Sky, a young man when he killed 18-Rabbit, was still alive when the 16th king of Copán, Yax Pasah, acceded to the throne and created three altars in the Great Plaza to further glorify 18-Rabbit.[17] It is not known for sure what relationship existed between the two cities at this time, but the beginning of the end for Copán had already set in. Yax Pasah did his best to declare his authority in the royal lineage by building Altar Q, which showed all the kings from Yax Kuk Mo down to himself. He may even have rewritten the history engraved on the Hieroglyphic Stairway to legitimize his claim and put himself in a better light.[18]

After Yax Pasah's death in AD 820, a 17th king took power, but was not able to save the city. Early in the ninth century, all ceremonial state functions ceased at Copán[19] and it was abandoned. The information we found is a bit contradictory at this point, but apparently the valley's population peak of 25,000 in the previous century did not decrease at this time; farming still continued and nobles held power in the areas surrounding the city center.[20] However, pollen studies indicate that by this time, most of the trees in the valley had been cut down.[21] This would explain the soil erosion that took place in the area, most likely

## "And It Came to Pass"

As at many other sites, we found examples of glyphs that can be translated as "it came to pass." They are found on some of the stelae in the Great Plaza. The glyphs can be a bit hard to recognize unless you are very familiar with their variations, so archaeological drawings are a good way to find them more easily. We recommend the chapter on Copán in Schele and Matthew's excellent *The Code of Kings* for detailed drawings of the stelae here and translations of many of their texts.

To find this phrase at Copán, the first place to go is Stela A, which has two examples of these glyphs. Facing the statue, there is an *utiy* on the right (north) side. It is in the left half of the third block from the bottom. Another one is on the back in the right column, just above the bottom row of glyphs. An *i-u-ti* can be seen in the bottom left corner of this text block. Stela C has an *utiya* in its column of glyphs. It can be found on the south side, on the left half of the sixth text block from the bottom. On the other side of the plaza, look at the back of Stela H. At the bottom is a section of hieroglyphs arranged in two columns. The

*(continued on page 145)*

*Looking for "it came to pass" on Stela A.*

143

For much of the evening, we checked out shops within walking distance of our hotel and the main plaza, looking at local handicrafts, clothing, and archaeological reproductions. There were a couple of shops selling all sorts of Mayan mementos, but we found some of the best items and deals with peddlers on the streets. We spent some time in a shop that had an Internet café, so email communication home was available. Later in the evening, we met up at a restaurant down the street from the hotel, the Llama del Bosque. This was suggested to us as a place to find good regional cuisine. The meal was quite good, with freshly blended fruit drinks and a hot, saucy dip of cheese and sausage before the main course. Apart from the loss of the room key, we quite enjoyed our evening in the delightful town of Copán Ruinas. There was a lot of activity going on, with delicious-smelling foods being cooked outside and many locals milling about on the streets. We wish we could have stayed longer.

The next morning, we packed up and drove out to the ruins. Although the site is very close to town, we had a bit of difficulty finding our way. The (continued on page 146)

*A view of the central plaza from our hotel*

diminishing the amount of crops harvested. Some palaces were burned and tombs looted during this period, so Copán's sudden decline was accompanied by some form of rebellion[22] or other internal discord.

Not much is known about any Postclassic history from Copán, but it was one of the first Classic Mayan cities to appear in European reports. It was mentioned as early as 1576 when Diego García de Palacio apparently describes it in a letter to Phillip II, king of Spain. Colonel Juan Galindo made an illustrated report of the site in 1834, but it was not published for many years.[23] Copán finally came to the attention of the general public after Stephens and Catherwood visited the site in 1839. The locals living near Copán knew of its existence but did not attach any value to the land or the ancient city and had no memory or legends of its past. John Stephens reports that no plans or drawings of Copán had been published, and they arrived hoping, but not expecting, to see something of interest.[24] The wonders they found and documented were far beyond anything they had seen in Mesoamerica at that time. Stephens attributes this lack of information to the ignorant and illiterate nature of the original Spanish conquerors and the fact that the Spanish government suppressed any information that could bring unwanted attention to their new possessions from other countries.[25]

Alfred Maudslay visited Copán in 1855, returning in 1894 to begin excavations and make drawings and molds of its monuments. These first expeditions were headed by the Peabody Museum, and more monuments and structures were found during this time, including the Hieroglyphic Stairway.[26] Between 1935 and 1946, Sylvanus Morley and the Carnegie Institute completed important excavation work, including partially restoring the blocks of the Hieroglyphic Stairway.[27] In the 1960s, the University of Pennsylvania continued work in the valley surrounding Copán, collecting valuable information on settlements in the rural areas. In 1985, the Honduran Archaeology and History Institute took over restoration and excavation work at the site.[28] William Fash from Northern Illinois University has been able to rebuild portions of the Hieroglyphic Stairway and interpret some of its record, publishing his findings in 1988.[29]

# BRIEF SITE OVERVIEW

From the entrance, we walked down a shady tree-lined path to a small guard's booth where we were greeted by bright red macaws. A short distance beyond is the Great Plaza, where most of Copán's famous stelae stand. Although it is an open, grassy field now, it was so densely covered with trees that in 1839 Stephens and Catherwood apparently did not find Structure 4 in the center of the plaza, although they meticulously explored and mapped the site.[30] This stepped, flat-topped pyramid is reminiscent of structures in such distant sites as Chichén Itzá and Teotihuacán and was built by Yax Kuk Mo or his son. A cache found here included a sacrificed jaguar and an offering pot containing pearls, jade, shells, cinnabar, and mercury.[31]

Spaced throughout the plaza are some of the magnificent stelae that are unique in the Mayan world. Here more than anywhere else, the sculpture approaches carving in the round; the larger-than-life figures seem almost ready to break free from their stony backgrounds. Aside from extremely talented artists, the reason for this unusual style is the type of rock

*("And It Came to Pass" continued)* left glyph of the top block of the right column reads *utiya*, but it may be too eroded to be readily identifiable.

Outside of the Great Plaza, there are what we believe to be three examples of this phrase on the west side of Stela J, right in the middle. There appear to be two *utiyas*, which can be translated as "it came to pass," and one *i-u-ti*, which can be translated as "and then it came to pass," all next to each other. There is also a glyph reading *utiya* on the west side of Stela 4. It is in the right column, second from the top, in the right half of the glyphic block. The left half is eroded. We suspect that more examples of these glyphs are at Copán, but these are all we have been able to find and they are quite enough for us.

*Inscription on the north side of Stela A which reads, "it came to pass, the stone was erected."*

## The Tree of Life

In one form or another, the world tree was perhaps the most important symbol to Mayan kings. It referred to the resurrection of the maize god, the creation of this current cycle, a connection from mortal life to the afterlife, and the path deceased kings took into the

*(continued on page 147)*

one-way streets around the Parque Central were a hindrance, but our main obstacle was a ravine on the east side of town, separating it from the ancient site. After a few dead ends, we eventually turned by a soccer field onto the correct road leading over the ravine. The short distance went by quickly, and not seeing any signs for Copán, we ended up driving past it. Not long afterward, we realized our mistake and turned around. We decided that a rather nondescript parking lot with tour buses must have been the entrance to the site, and we were right. So when in doubt, look for the buses.

The ticket booth was in a modern visitor center surrounding a large reproduction of Copán in its heyday. It was here that we got our first unpleasant surprise in Honduras. Accustomed to the entrance fees for sites in Mexico and Guatemala, we were not prepared for how much we had to pay. For non-nationals, the cost was about US $15. Entrance to the onsite museum was extra, so the total for both was over US $22 per person, and they would not accept credit cards or foreign currency. The guidebooks had not given such high amounts, so be forewarned and take extra cash. Pooling our lempiras, we had just enough to enter the site, so we had to skip the museum, which has some great exhibits. Luckily, we had visited the small archaeological museum on the other side of the plaza from our hotel earlier that morning. The fee was quite reasonable and they had a nice collection of sculpture and artifacts from Copán, as well as displays of ancient tombs from the area.

the Maya found in this region. The volcanic andesite found locally was better suited to this volumetric approach than the limestone used at most other Mayan cities, where monumental sculpture was usually done in low relief.[32] Just about all of the stelae in the plaza represent 18-Rabbit and are generally thought to have been commissioned during his reign. An exception is Stela E, which depicts Waterlily Jaguar, Copán's seventh king. It was moved from its original location and then placed on the late Classic Structure 1 on the western edge of the plaza. In addition to being removed, Waterlilly Jaguar's face has also been chipped off,[33] so a later king really wanted to assert his own authority and view of history. We suspect 18-Rabbit.

A common motif found in his monuments is that of royal power and celestial symbols.[34] The stelae depict 18-Rabbit in the guise of various gods, with imagery connecting his authority to them. Most have hieroglyphic inscriptions commemorating important dates and events. Their appearance is strangely eastern and they would not look out of place in settings as far away as Angkor Wat, Cambodia. Each stela was built over a cross-shaped vault, oriented to the cardinal directions. They contained caches of jade, shell, and gold or tumbaga (a copper/gold alloy) and are of a later date.[35] Does this mean that the stelae were erected after 18-Rabbit's death? Or were the vaults added later? There is no definitive answer yet.

Currently, the only open vault that can be seen is at the foot of Stela A. This monument shows 18-Rabbit with an important mat headdress, but its meaning is unclear.[36] It may be a local version of the mat pattern symbol of divine authority that is commonly seen in one form or another in many Mayan sites. A row of glyphs runs down either side, as well as a double row on the back. Among the writings on the south side are title glyphs for the kings of Tikal, Calakmul, and Palenque, in addition to Copán,[37] where 18-Rabbit is obviously referring to himself. There is no protective covering on this stela, leading us to guess that it might be a replica. Several molds of stelae here have been made; a replica of Stela A stands outside the Peabody Museum at Harvard.

A bit to the north is Stela B. This carving shows 18-Rabbit wearing a turban-like headdress that appears to be unique to Copán. Many of its kings are depicted wearing this headdress, but why Copán would have its own form of headgear unlike any other Mayan site is unknown. 18-Rabbit has a small symbolic beard and his face looks quite different from the carving on Stela A. Although the top of the monument is eroded above the turban are two shapes, one on each side, that look surprisingly like elephant trunks at first glance. LDS visitors might be tempted to imagine that they are looking at proof of the Book of Mormon's authenticity, but we highly doubt that the eighth-century Maya in Honduras had any direct knowledge of elephants. Much more likely is that these shapes are three-dimensional representations of the glyph *mo*, the Mayan word for "macaw,"

*(The Tree of Life continued)* heavens and their own resurrection. Kings and nobles all over the ancient Mayan world had themselves depicted with this tree as a sign of their divine authority and right to rule. The imagery that represented the tree was quite diverse: crosses, serpents, flowering vines and fruit, a stalk of maize, and even the Milky Way.

At Copán, another image is added to the list: that of a crocodile. These symbols are found on aprons worn by 18-Rabbit on some of the stelae in the Great Plaza. Stela A has serpent branches on its apron and Stela C shows a crocodile tree emerging from a crack in a mountain, both referring to the world tree. In fact, both sides of Stela C have some form of the world tree on their aprons and Stela B has a world tree apron as well.[53] Stela D has six serpents on its sides. "Six snakes" is *wakah kan* in Mayan, which also means "raised-up sky," another name for the world tree.[54] Symbols on the west side of Stela C proclaim 18-Rabbit to be king and "tree lord."[55] The crocodile tree was considered home to Itzam-Ye,[56] a divine bird symbolizing Itzamná, a benevolent creator deity worshipped in the Yucatán, who has many Christlike characteristics. This symbol, also called the principal bird deity, can be seen on cross-shaped tree carvings at Palenque and Yaxchilán. We also found it interesting that the Mayan term for soul was *sak nik*, meaning "white flower," and they considered their souls to be flowers on the sacred world tree.[57]

*(continued on page 149)*

147

representing a symbolic macaw mountain.[38]

Next in line is Stela C. This unusual carving has two images of 18-Rabbit; a young version faces east to the rising sun and an older, bearded version faces west to the setting sun. On the eastern side, a design of twisted ropes represents an umbilical reaching to the heavens, a symbol of the king's divine authority. A turtle is carved into the western façade, symbolizing the cosmic turtle and the crack in the earth through which the maize god arose after his resurrection. Since the setting sun was a symbol for the end of life, 18-Rabbit may have wanted to stress his belief in resurrection, but whether his own or that of a god or ancestor is not known.[39]

While we were gazing at the traces of red paint still visible on the stela, we overheard a site guide leading a tourist couple and pointing at details on the stone with a long pole topped with a feather. For some reason, he was explaining burial practices to them. Although it would probably be frowned upon, one of us nonchalantly came closer to hear what he was saying (this is a good way to get interesting tidbits of information without actually paying for a tour). He was telling them that the Maya, both modern and ancient, distinguished between burying adults and children. According to him, a child under eight years old was considered pure and buried facing a different direction than someone who had died at an older age. Not everything the ancient Maya believed about what happened after death is known. Kings had a definite expectation of resurrection and deification, but there is evidence that the common people had a belief in an

afterlife as well. Bodies were carefully laid out in graves, pointing either north or west, which were considered the directions of otherworldly realms. Regardless of class or status, corn meal was usually placed in the deceased person's mouth, along with a jade bead, symbolizing breath and life.[40]

Other stelae and altars are located in the Great Plaza. They all exhibit a high level of craftsmanship and each is interesting on its own, including an altar that is one of the first known representations of a serpent with legs,[41] but we will just give a further mention to Stela H. It faces Stela A from across the plaza and the two are considered to be a pair. For a long time, Stela H was thought to represent a woman because of its long beaded skirt.[42] It is now believed to be another image of 18-Rabbit, this time in the guise of the maize god or perhaps the first father.[43] As for Pakal and his son at Palenque, the jade skirt is a symbol of the maize god's resurrection and by extension, that of the king as well, just one of the symbols of fertility and resurrection on this stela.[44] In the vault in front, a cache containing the earliest example of gold among the Maya was found. The gold objects date to AD 730 and like other Mayan gold, came from Panama or Columbia.[45] To the east, the plaza opens up and a path leads to Las Sepulturas, a residential area for common people that has been excavated and is open to visitors. Not far from the plaza along this path, Stela J marks the border of the ceremonial precinct, with one side carved with symbols of the king's divine authority and the other denoting the residential area.[46]

South from the Great Plaza is the ballcourt, one of the best preserved in all of Mesoamerica.

*(The Tree of Life continued)* The reverence and importance given by the Maya, both ancient and modern, to the world tree approaches that of the Christian world toward the cross. In fact, the two symbols have become closely intertwined since the introduction of Christianity in Mesoamerica. Fortunately for evangelizing Catholic priests, many Christian doctrines easily fit in with ancient Mayan beliefs. Kinich Ahaw, a sun god known as Our Father Sun, was identified with God the Father; Hunapu, the maize god who was killed in the underworld and then resurrected, became Jesus Christ.[58] See the chapter on Palenque for an in-depth discussion of the topic of Mayan deities and the sacred world tree. We make no definite claims, but there do appear to be grains of doctrinal truth in the origins of these Mayan beliefs. It is possible that teachings from Book of Mormon prophets about the tree of life and the Savior's crucifixion on a cross endured among Mesoamerican people and were eventually woven into Mayan concepts of their origin and deities.

## Succession of Kings

Altar Q is perhaps the best example of the importance of a line of authority to a king's rulership. Yax Pasah, Copán's 16th king, built it to trace his authority back through the centuries to the dynasty's founder, Yax Kuk Mo. He even has his image facing Yax Kuk Mo, receiving emblems of kingship directly from him in the form of royal scepters. Judging from many monuments and texts from the entire Mayan region, it is easy to see that

*(continued on page 151)*

Macaw-shaped stone markers can be seen here. The court seems to be divided into thirds, but little is known about how the Mayan game was really played. The ballcourt forms the northern edge of the Plaza of the Hieroglyphic Stairway. While 18-Rabbit began the stairway, it was completed in AD 756 by Copán's 15th king and contains 2,200 glyphs carved into its blocks, comprising the longest text known in the Mayan world.[47] Efforts continue to decipher it, but erosion and the fact that many of the blocks have fallen out of place may make that goal almost impossible to reach. It is worth noting that the text on the left half of the stairway is carved in a Teotihuacán style of writing,[48] showing a further link to central Mexico. This side may be a duplication of the Mayan glyphs on the right side, but that is not known for sure. Currently, the stairway is covered by a long green tarp, which offers some protection from the elements. The ornately carved Stela M stands in front.

The Hieroglyphic Stairway is part of an enormous complex of pyramids, platforms, and royal buildings that included residences for the kings and nobles, as well as their graves. The eastern edge of these structures has been washed away through the centuries by the Copán River that used to run along the edge of the city. There is more to see at the site, but we finished up in the West Patio. A pyramid known as Structure 16 defines its eastern edge. Archaeologists tunneling into it found an ornately painted and stuccoed temple underneath, known as the Rosalila. Unlike the visible structures at Copán, it has been perfectly preserved by the construction on top of it. A reconstruction of it is in the site museum, so if you have enough money, it is probably worth seeing. The door to the tunnel is visible at the ground level, but it was locked. Some guidebooks may mention that you can be taken inside to see the actual Rosalila, but we did not see anyone around offering to let us in.

What we came to see in this plaza is a carving known as Altar Q (actually a replica). It is likely that what are now called altars were once used as thrones. This one was built by Yax Pasah and shows him and the 15 kings before him, wrapped around the altar's sides. The line of authority starts with Yax Kuk Mo and since the carving ends where it began, Yax Pasah is shown facing Yax Kuk Mo, receiving his authority directly from the dynastic founder. The text on top refers to the founding of the dynasty with the "arrival" of Yax Kuk Mo and gives him a title of Ruler of the West.[49] At its dedication, Yax Pasah had 15 jaguars sacrificed at this spot, one for every king before him.[50] More than any other monument we have seen, Altar Q shows the importance of succession to Mayan kings and how they viewed their authority as passing from one to another. Each king is identified by a glyph or other symbol. As an interesting sidenote, 18-Rabbit's father Smoke Jaguar is shown seated on a glyph meaning "five katun." He is sometimes referred to as "Five-Katun Lord" because he lived during five *katunob*. A *katun* is a period of time defined by the Maya as 20 years of 360 days each, or 19.7 of our modern years. Ukit Took, the 17th king of Copán, tried to build his own version of Altar Q (known as Altar L), showing him receiving authority from Yax Pasah. It was poorly carved and never even finished,[51] so it seems obvious that the dynasty fell and the royal center was abandoned during his interrupted reign.

*(Succession of Kings continued)* a king's position and authority depended on his depiction with royal symbols and establishing a relationship with gods and past kings. Many kings took royal names had by previous kings. Names that include Balam (jaguar), Pakal (shield), and Chan (sky) are common. In addition, each city's rulers tend to have a set of names particular to that region. Another common practice was to take the name of Kinich, the sun god, or Itzamná, the benevolent creator god.[59]

It is curious that the Book of Mormon mentions so many kings, when kings are not known as part of the Native American culture Joseph Smith or his associates would have been familiar with. Although Nephi declines to be a king and warns of their danger, Jacob 1:11 tells us that those who ruled after him were called kings and took his name in remembrance, becoming Nephi II, Nephi III, and so forth. This era of their history was referred to as the reign of kings. The Nephites had many kings throughout their history. After a system of judges replaced royal rulers, ambitious leaders emerged from time to time in an attempt to overthrow the government and set themselves up as kings once again. By comparing these accounts to the ancient history of Mesoamerica, we see that they fit in quite easily, including the political machinations and intrigue that plagued the reigns of so many Book of Mormon kings.

# Foreign Kings

Yax Kuk Mo, the founder of Copán's ruling dynasty, was an outsider to this valley and the people who had been living here. He was a Mayan noble from a distant city that became king over a non-Mayan people, the Lenca. What happened in AD 426 and how could he have established such a dynasty that ruled successfully for centuries? Did he conquer the Copán Valley by force, or by some subtler means? Was his lineage a deciding factor? Did he have some other symbols of authority that convinced the Lenca? We may never know exactly how he did it, but we do know that he did.

The Book of Mormon has similar stories of kings who became accepted rulers over groups of people who were essentially foreigners to them. Omni 18 tells how Mosiah, a prophet among the Nephites, fled the city of Nephi with his righteous followers. They eventually found the people of Zarahemla and joined them. Mosiah became their king, although the Nephites were certainly a minority and had no way of forcing the issue. Why would the people of Zarahemla (sometimes called the Mulekites) accept this unknown outsider as their king? Although both groups claimed to be from Jerusalem, Zarahemla and his people had kept no records and he could only give his lineage from memory, perhaps forgetting some of his ancestors. Their language had become corrupted, or most likely, evolved to resemble the indigenous languages spoken around them. They had no visible emblems of royal authority; Zarahemla was not even referred to as a king. In contrast, Mosiah kept written records proving his descent from Jerusalem. He also had objects of divine authority like the Urim and Thummim and the Liahona. The people in the land of Zarahemla probably welcomed someone who could establish an authentic ruling dynasty with the proper credentials. The fact that Mosiah was a righteous prophet of God was another bonus.

Outsiders could become kings by devious means as well in the Book of Mormon. Alma 47 recounts how Amalickiah, a Nephite dissenter who unsuccessfully tried to establish himself as a king among his own people, fled to the Lamanites to stir up trouble. He concocted a plot to ingratiate himself with the Lamanite armies and overthrow their current king. He was able to impress the Lamanite king Lehonti and was appointed as second leader over the army. A servant of his slowly poisoned Lehonti so that he eventually died. Then Amalickiah was made king, as was the Lamanite custom. In verse 35, he even marries Lehonti's widow and through his fraud was proclaimed king throughout all the land of Nephi. These stories of outsiders being readily accepted as kings over people who were not their own may have seemed far-fetched at one time, but actual Mesoamerican history is evidence that such events were plausible.

*Yax Pasah (right), 16th king of Copán, symbolically receiving a staff of diving authority to rule from Yax Kuk Mo (left), founder of the dynasty.*

# Lunar Cycles of Time

The ancient Maya were experts in watching the skies and measuring time by astronomical events. They had extremely complex calendars formed by the cyclical interlocking of years of different duration. These calendars could be used to formulate dates thousands of years into the past or the future. Mayan priests understood the movements of heavenly bodies and could predict their positions with accuracy.

Phases of the moon were one of the cycles they used to measure time.[60] We usually think of the lunar cycle as occurring once per month, but it actually lasts a bit over 29.5 days. The Maya realized that the lunar cycle lasted between 29 and 30 days, but since they had no system of decimal points, they devised another correction for the errors that would inevitably creep into their long-term calendars.[61] That they used completed lunar cycles as a means for recording the passage of time is evident from the hieroglyphic text found on the north side of Stela A. Near the middle of the column are two text blocks that read, "Fifteen days after the moon arrived, six moons had ended."[62]

Apparently, the Nephites used a similar method for reckoning time. In Omni 20–21, an account is given of an event that took place during the reign of the first King Mosiah in Zarahemla. The people found Coriantumr, last of the Jaredites. The text relates that he remained with them in Zarahemla for nine moons. If the Book of Mormon were a modern invention, we might expect it to say "nine months," but the Nephites were using a valid ancient system of measuring time by the visible phases of the moon, rather than the rather arbitrary modern system of months.

# Deforestation

Today, the Copán Valley is lush and green, thickly covered with forest. But in the ninth century, most of the trees in this area had been cut down. Although monumental buildings were made out of stone, trees were a crucial resource in densely populated areas, both for residential buildings and for the production of stucco. It might be hard to imagine now, but many of these cities probably turned into urban sprawl, with dense populations crowding into areas that had been cleared of all trees and vegetation. Stone, cement, and stucco covered the landscape in the population centers. In this area, the deforestation was so severe that it caused soil erosion, which may have had negative effects on food production.

The Book of Mormon describes what appear to be similar environmental impacts from large populations. In chapter 3 of Helaman, a great number of dissenters left Zarahemla and traveled northward. We are not told the reason for their departure, but overpopulation may have been a factor. According to verse 5, they eventually settled in a far away region with many lakes and rivers that had been denuded of timber by previous inhabitants. Whether these were Jaredites, Nephites, or some culture recognized by traditional archaeology is not known, but this example of large scale deforestation follows a pattern seen centuries later at Copán and many other Mayan sites.

# Putting It All Together

This book has only scratched the surface to understanding the Mayan world. We continue to learn new things about this culture almost monthly. Archaeology in Mesoamerica is still relatively young compared to other parts of the world. Over the past 50 years, much of what was believed about the Maya has been completely overturned. What we now know today is completely opposite of what was known previously, and most of that knowledge pertains to cultures and eras from after the close of the Book of Mormon. We saw literally hundreds of unexcavated ruins on our drives or even during casual hikes in the forests of Mexico and Guatemala. Who knows what excavations at these sites (if they ever happen) will bring? New discoveries have continued to make the case for the Book of Mormon taking place in Mesoamerica stronger than before, especially as more work is done on Preclassic sites dating to the Book of Mormon time periods. We look foreword to what the next 50 years will bring and will be ever watchful.

Learning about the Mayan culture and visiting the ruins of Mexico, Guatemala, and Honduras are valuable in their own right. This was an amazing culture, and their achievements rival those that occurred with the other great civilizations in Europe and Asia at the time. We greatly value our experience interacting with the local people in our trips and gaining an understanding and appreciation of a culture different from our own. We have plans to return to these areas as they are dear to our hearts and we now have a greater understanding of the sites we visited than when we were there. When we return, we have things to look for that we missed the first time.

By no means is this the end of our study. There are many more sites in Mesoamerica that can easily be visited, many of which have interesting comparisons to the Book of Mormon. In fact, in our travels we visited more sites and have amassed many fascinating details, too much for a single book. Much of this information came from our travels through the Yucatán Peninsula in Mexico, where we visited ruins such as Chichén Itzá, Uxmal, Becán, and Calakmul. We had many worthwhile experiences on that trip and discovered many similarities to accounts from the Book of Mormon in these areas. Sadly, we were not able to fit it all into this book, but even now we are working on a second volume of our adventures, which focuses on our expedition to the Yucatán and the sites we visited along the way.

In this next book we will share details about what we learned concerning the artifacts and archaeological record of that region, much of which is not widely discussed. We have seen and handled gold plates with Mayan hieroglyphic writing that

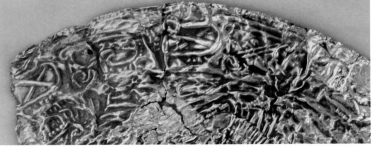

*Yes, there actually are gold plates with writing on them from Mesoamerica.*

have been archived in the Peabody Museum at Harvard for almost a century. We have explored defensive fortifications erected to protect cities from attack and invasion, including massive stone walls and earthworks that almost perfectly match Captain Moroni's effective defenses. We descended into caves where unfossilized pre-Columbian horse bones have been found among ceramic artifacts. We researched the origins of the legends of Quetzalcoatl to see how traces can be found all throughout Mesoamerican cultures.

We look forward to detailing our travels, the results of our study, and many more sites in our next book. Even though most sites in this area are probably outside of lands mentioned in the Book of Mormon, the Yucatán is well worth the visit and it is much more accessible to tourists than many areas of Guatemala. We hope to take additional trips to other regions, perhaps to central Mexico to look at even more ancient Olmec and Zapotec sites. The Pacific coast of Guatemala and Mexico is another candidate, as it contained very early settlements from the Preclassic period and is most likely where Lehi's group landed in the Promised Land.

We believe over time that the evidence will continue to tilt more in favor of the Book of Mormon, but most likely only to a point. There is a limit to the applicability of non-LDS scholars' opinions regarding evidence for this unique book of scripture. It should go without saying that they are not going to believe it or accept evidences that support it. As an example, Michael Coe is a renowned archaeologist and expert on the Maya, and someone whose work we greatly admire. He was interviewed for a recent Frontline documentary on the LDS Church shown on PBS and stated that there was not any archaeological evidence for the Book of Mormon in Mesoamerica. He also stated that there was no archaeological justification for the Exodus and other accounts in the Old Testament from biblical lands. We actually think his comments were fair; there is no hard evidence that proves our beliefs. Golden or brass plates with reformed Egyptian writing on them, religious practice of the law of Moses, or a city called Zarahemla are yet to be found. It is the archaeologists' job to come up with the best theory based only on what is known through the current archaeological record. They are forced to paint a broad story of ancient civilizations, often with very little specific information. The scientific method is required for this process and we respect this. But as we have seen over the years, these theories are fluid and ever-changing, sometimes dramatically. We do not expect science to ever prove or disprove the Book of Mormon. As we read in scriptural accounts, faith must be developed and is essential to attain this knowledge; proving the Book of Mormon empirically most likely is not a part of God's plan.

What we are saying here is that the events described in its pages are plausible and could have happened in Mesoamerican regions. Given a good understanding of what it really says, there is nothing here that disproves the Book of Mormon. There is no way that Joseph Smith could have known that major civilizations like the Maya or the Olmec existed in the new world. To make the claims he did was outrageous for his time, even much more so than they seem today. We forget that many of the previous arguments against the Book of Mormon have been discarded as they are no longer valid. It is true that we have not found evidence for every controversial item in its account and we probably never will. But that should not weaken our faith, for at the end of it all, this is what will bring us to a knowledge of the truth of the Book of Mormon. What we have learned through this process of study, preparation, travel, and writing has strengthened our faith in this scriptural record, but it is no substitute. We have learned and grown much more than we ever would have expected from our trips to these lands. Seeing these sites in person and studying what really went on here have given us a greater appreciation for the Book of Mormon and probably a more accurate understanding for what really happened. Our faith has grown because of our experiences, but a true knowledge of the Book of Mormon's truthfulness is only obtained through personal revelation from the divine. We hope to continue traveling and studying the field of Mesoamerican archaeology, but the spiritual aspect of our study will always be paramount.

# SITE TIMELINE

*All dates are approximate.*

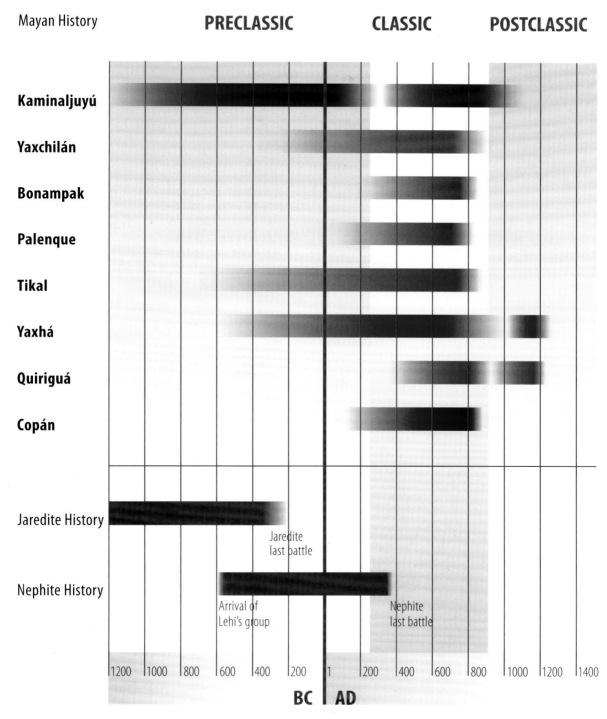

Mayan History · **PRECLASSIC** · **CLASSIC** · **POSTCLASSIC**

Kaminaljuyú

Yaxchilán

Bonampak

Palenque

Tikal

Yaxhá

Quiriguá

Copán

Jaredite History

Jaredite
last battle

Nephite History

Arrival of
Lehi's group

Nephite
last battle

1200 1000 800 600 400 200 1 200 400 600 800 1000 1200 1400

**BC AD**

# EXPLANATION OF EMBLEM GLYPHS

Most texts at Kaminaljuyú were destroyed anciently and no emblem glyph has survived.

Yaxchilán has two emblem glyphs. The first one means "split sky."

We have found two different emblem glyphs for Bonampak.

Three emblem glyphs are known for Palenque. The first means "bone."

The city itself was referred to with this glyph meaning "great water."

Toktan, the third glyph, is an early name for Palenque and may refer to the kingdom's capital.

Tikal's emblem glyph is knot of tied hair.

Yaxhá's emblem glyph is a phonetic spelling of its ancient name, "blue-green water."

Quiriguá's emblem glyph is a representation of a cacao tree.

Copán's emblem glyph is a picture of a bat's head.

# PRONUNCIATION GUIDE

| | |
|---|---|
| Atitlán | ah-teet-**LAHN** |
| bajo | **BAH**-ho |
| Bonampak | bo-nahm-**PAHK** |
| Calakmul | kah-lahk-**MOOL** |
| Campeche | kahm-**PEH**-cheh |
| cenote | seh-**NO**-teh |
| Chichén Itzá | chee-**CHEN** eet-**SAH** |
| Copán | co-**PAHN** |
| Co-op Bethel | coe-**OPE** beh-**TEL** |
| Corozal | co-ro-**SAHL** |
| Grijalva | gree-**HAHL**-vah |
| Itzamná | eet-sahm-**NAH** |
| Izapa | ee-**SAH**-pah |
| katun | kah-**TOON** |
| Kaminaljuyú | kah-mee-nahl-hoo-**YOO** |
| Naranjo | nah-**RAHN**-ho |
| Pacaya | pah-**KAH**-yah |
| Palenque | pah-**LEHN**-keh |
| Panajachel | pah-nah-hah-**CHEL** |
| Petén | peh-**TEN** |
| Quetzalcoatl | ket-sahl-co-**ATL** |
| Quiriguá | kee-ree-**GWAH** |
| sacbé | sahk-**BEH** |
| Sayaxché | sigh-yahsh-**CHE** |
| Sololá | so-lo-**LAH** |
| Teotihuacán | teh-o-tee-wah-**KAHN** |
| Tikal | tee-**KAHL** |
| Tulum | too-**LOOM** |
| Uaxactún | wah-shahk-**TOON** |
| Usumacinta | oo-soo-mah-**SEEN**-tah |
| Xibalba | shee-**BAHL**-bah |
| Yaxchilán | yahsh-chee-**LAHN** |
| Yaxhá | yahsh-**HAH** |

# Suggested Books and Websites

Diego de Landa, *Yucatan Before and After the Conquest*

John L. Stephens, *Incidents of Travel in Central America, Chiapas, and Yucatan*, vol. I and II

John L. Stephens, *Incidents of Travel in Yucatan*, vol. 1 and II

Simon Martin and Nikolai Grube, *Chronicle of the Maya Kings and Queens*

Michael D. Coe, *The Maya*

Linda Schele and Peter Mathews, *The Code of Kings*

Robert J. Sharer with Loa P. Traxler, *The Ancient Maya*

Lynn V. Foster, *Handbook to Life in the Ancient Maya World*

Andrew Coe, *Archaeological Mexico*

John L. Sorenson, *Images of Ancient America, Visualizing Book of Mormon Life*

Jerry Ainsworth, *The Lives and Travels of Mormon and Moroni*

Joseph L. Allen, *Exploring the Lands of the Book of Mormon*


http://www.peabody.harvard.edu/col/browse.cfm

http://www.mesoweb.com/

http://www.famsi.org/

http://mayaruins.com/yucmap.html

http://www.delange.org/Default/CentralAmerica2/CentralAmerica2.htm

# ENDNOTES

## 1 - Why Go to Mesoamerica?

1. See Orson Pratt, *Journal of Discourses,* 14:324-31.
2. John L. Stephens, *Incidents of Travel in Central America, Chiapas, and Yucatan* (New York: Dover Publications, 1969), 1:97.
3. Ibid., 2:295-98.
4. *Times and Seasons,* 3:927.
5. Andrew Coe, *Archaeological Mexico* (Emeryville: Avalon Travel Publishing, 2001), 309-10.
6. See John L. Sorenson, *An Ancient American Setting for the Book of Mormon* (Salt Lake City: Deseret Book, 1996); Joseph L. Allen, *Exploring the Lands of the Book of Mormon* (Orem: S.A. Publishers, 1989); and Paul R. Cheesman, *The World of the Book of Mormon* (Salt Lake City: Deseret Book, 1978).
7. Sorenson, *An Ancient American Setting for the Book of Mormon,* 8-23.
8. *Engineering an Empire, The Maya: Death Empire,* documentary, A&E Television Networks, 2006.
9. Simon Martin and Nikolai Grube, *Chronicle of the Maya Kings and Queens* (London: Thames & Hudson, 2000), 9.
10. Ibid., 52-53.
11. Allen, *Exploring the Lands of the Book of Mormon,* 55-67.
12. Ibid., and John L. Sorenson, *Images of Ancient America, Visualizing Book of Mormon Life* (Provo: Research Press, 1998), 216.
13. Rebecca B. González Lauck, "El Preclásico Medio en Mesoamérica," *Arqueología Mexicana,* vol. VIII, num. 45 (Sept.-Oct. 2000), 15.
14. For example, see John Montgomery, *Dictionary of Maya Hieroglyphs* (New York: Hippocrene Books, 2002).
15. Diego de Landa, *Yucatan Before and After the Conquest* (New York: Dover Publications, 1978), iii.
16. Ibid., 82.
17. Ibid., 8.
18. Ibid., 33.
19. Ibid., 42-43.
20. Ibid., 50.
21. Ibid., 71.
22. Ibid., 85-86, 90.
23. See Michel Graulich, "Entre el Mito y la Historia," *Arqueología Mexicana,* vol. VIII, num. 45 (Sept.-Oct. 2000), 78; Peter D. Harrison, *The Lords of Tikal* (London: Thames & Hudson, 1999), 92.
24. John Montgomery, *Tikal an Illustrated History of the Ancient Maya Capital* (New York: Hippocrene Books, 2001), 8.
25. Landa, *Yucatan Before and After the Conquest,* 85.

## 2 - The Book's Purpose

1. Stephen D. Douglas, personal communication (email) 2006.
2. Andrew Coe, *Archaeological Mexico* (Chico: Moon Publications, 1998), 339-40.

## 4 - Kaminaljuyú

1. Robert J. Sharer with Loa P. Traxler, *The Ancient Maya* (Stanford: Stanford University Press, 2006), 194.
2. Ibid., 195.
3. Ibid.

4. Ibid., 35, 83.
5. Lynn V. Foster, *Handbook to Life in the Ancient Maya World* (New York: Oxford University Press, 2005), 122.
6. Ibid., 95.
7. Ibid., 30; Sharer with Traxler, *The Ancient Maya*, 703.
8. Sharer with Traxler, *The Ancient Maya*, 235; Foster, *Handbook to Life in the Ancient Maya World*, 109.
9. Foster, *Handbook to Life in the Ancient Maya World*, 31.
10. See Michael D. Coe, *The Maya* (New York: Thames & Hudson Inc, 2005), 74-76; Sharer with Traxler, *The Ancient Maya*, 196, 232.
11. See Coe, *The Maya*, 53-55, 72.
12. Foster, *Handbook to Life in the Ancient Maya World*, 277.
13. Ibid., 35.
14. Ibid., 42.
15. Ibid., 46; Coe, *The Maya*, 90.
16. Jeremy A. Sabloff, *The New Archaeology and the Ancient Maya* (New York: W. H. Freeman and Company, 1990), 101.
17. Coe, *The Maya*, 90.
18. Foster, *Handbook to Life in the Ancient Maya World*, 49.
19. Ibid., 109.
20. Sharer with Traxler, *The Ancient Maya*, 83.
21. Ibid., 195.
22. Ibid., 235.
23. Foster, *Handbook to Life in the Ancient Maya World*, 38.
24. See Joseph L. Allen, *Exploring the Lands of the Book of Mormon* (Orem: S.A. Publishers, 1989), 359-70; John L. Sorenson, *An Ancient American Setting for the Book of Mormon* (Salt Lake City: Deseret Book, 1996); 141-48; and F. Richard Hauck, *Deciphering the Geography of the Book of Mormon* (Salt Lake City: Deseret Book, 1988), 163.
25. David F. Mora-Marín, "Kaminaljuyu Stela 10 Script Classification and Linguistic Affiliation," *Ancient America,* 16 (Cambridge University Press, 2005), 79.
26. Coe, *The Maya*, 74.
27. Foster, *Handbook to Life in the Ancient Maya World*, 277.
28. Ibid., 275.
29. Ibid., 41.
30. Mora-Marín, *Ancient America,* 16, 72-75.
31. Ibid., 66.
32. Ibid., 64, 66.
33. Marion Popenoe de Hatch, Erick Ponciano, Tomas Barrientos Q., Mark Brenner, and Charles Ortloff, "Climate and Technological Innovation at Kaminaljuyu, Guatemala," *Ancient America,* 13 (Cambridge University Press, 2002), 109.
34. Jim Scott, "CU-Boulder Archaeology Team Discovers First Ancient Manioc Fields in Americas." Onine. <http://colorado.edu/news/releases/2007/305.html>; accessed Jan. 13, 2008.
35. David Jacobs and Glen E. Rice, "Hohokam Impacts on the Vegetation of Canal System Two, Phoenix Basin," *Anthropological Field Studies Number 42* (Arizona State University, 2002), 4-6.

# 6 ~ The Pacaya Volcano

1. Robert J. Sharer with Loa P. Traxler, *The Ancient Maya* (Stanford University Press, 2006), 35.
2. Jeremy A. Sabloff, *The New Archaeology and the Ancient Maya* (New York: W. H. Freeman and Company, 1990), 116.
3. Sharer with Traxler, *The Ancient Maya*, 507.
4. Ibid.

5.  Payson D. Sheets, "Tropical Time Capsule," *Secrets of the Maya* (Long Island City: Hatherleigh Press, 2003), 48–49.
6.  Ibid.; Sharer with Traxler, *The Ancient Maya*, 280–81.
7.  Mary Miller and Karl Taube, *An Illustrated Dictionary of the Gods and Symbols of Ancient Mexico and the Maya* (London: Thames & Hudson Ltd, 1993), 18.
8.  Ted Chamberlain, *National Geographic News*. Online. <http://news.nationalgeographic.com/news/2007/02/070226-sinkhole-photo.html>; accessed Jan. 8. 2008.

# 7 - Lake Atitlán

1.  Karla J. Cardona Caravantes, *Arqueología, Etnohistoria y Conflictos de Tierra en la Región Sur del Lago de Atitlán* (Guatemala City: Universidad del Valle de Guatemala, 2002), 8–9.
2.  See Joseph L. Allen, *Exploring the Lands of the Book of Mormon* (Orem: S.A. Publishers, 1989), 240, 324–25; John L. Sorenson, *An Ancient American Setting for the Book of Mormon* (Salt Lake City: Deseret Book, 1996), 176–77.
3.  Nancy Avendaño, "Arqueologia para Buzos," *Revista Domingo,* no. 1056 (19 August 2001), 9.
4.  Ibid.
5.  Ibid., 10; Guillermo Mata Amado, "Exploraciones Subacuáticas en los Lagos de Guatemala," *XV Simposio de Investigaciones Arqueológicas en Guatemala,* (Guatemala: Museo Nacional de Arqueología y Etnología, 2001), 594.
6.  See John L. Sorenson, *An Ancient American Setting for the Book of Mormon* (Salt Lake City: Deseret Book, 1996), 176, 222–25.

# 9 - Yaxchilán

1.  Linda Schele and Peter Mathews, *The Code of Kings* (New York: Simon & Schuster, 1998), 363; Peter Mathews, "Epigrafía de la Región del Usumacinta," *Arqueología Mexicana*, vol. IV, num. 22 (Nov.-Dec. 1996), 15.
2.  Andrew Coe, *Archaeological Mexico* (Chico: Moon Publications, 1998), 247.
3.  Simon Martin and Nikolai Grube, *Chronicle of the Maya Kings and Queens* (London: Thames & Hudson, 2000), 118–19.
4.  Mathews, *Arqueología Mexicana*, 39.
5.  Martin and Grube, *Chronicle of the Maya Kings and Queens*, 123.
6.  Lynn V. Foster, *Handbook to Life in the Ancient Maya World* (New York: Oxford University Press, 2005), 288.
7.  Martin and Grube, *Chronicle of the Maya Kings and Queens*, 123.
8.  Ibid., 226–27.
9.  Ibid., 128.
10. Foster, *Handbook to Life in the Ancient Maya World*, 290.
11. Coe, *Archaeological Mexico*, 248.
12  Ibid.
13. Martin and Grube, *Chronicle of the Maya Kings and Queens*, 128–29.
14. Coe, *Archaeological Mexico*, 248.
15. Mathews, *Arqueología Mexicana*, 21.
16. Coe, *Archaeological Mexico*, 249.
17. Ibid.
18. Ibid., 250.
19. Ibid., 250-52.
20. Ibid., 252.
21. Martin and Grube, *Chronicle of the Maya Kings and Queens*, 124.

22. Michael D. Coe, *The Maya* (New York: Thames & Hudson Inc., 2005), 162.
23. Carolyn E. Tate, *Yaxchilan: The Design of a Maya Ceremonial City* (Austin: University of Texas Press, 1992), 68-69.
24. Coe, *Archaeological Mexico*, 257.
25. Ibid., 254-55.
26. Ian Graham and Eric von Euw, *Corpus of the Maya Hieroglyphic Inscriptions,* pt. 1 (Cambridge: Peabody Museum, 1977), 3:10.
27. Tom Gidwitz, "Pioneers of the Bajo," *Secrets of the Maya* (Long Island City: Hatherleigh Press, 2003), 174.
28. T. Patrick Culbert, "The New Maya," *Secrets of the Maya*, 5.
29. Jeremy A. Sabloff, *The New Archaeology and the Ancient Maya* (New York: W. H. Freeman and Company, 1990), 94.
30. Ibid., 93.
31. See Foster, *Handbook to Life in the Ancient Maya World*, 288-89.
32. John L. Sorenson, *An Ancient American Setting for the Book of Mormon* (Salt Lake City: Deseret Book, 1996), 46-47.
33. F. Richard Hauk, *Deciphering the Geography of the Book of Mormon* (Salt Lake City: Deseret Book Company, 1988), 121.
34. Joseph L. Allen, *Exploring the Lands of the Book of Mormon* (Orem, Utah: S.A. Publishers, 1989).
35. See Mathews, *Arqueología Mexicana*, 18-19.
36. See Schele and Mathews, *The Code of Kings*, 132 and Foster, *Handbook to Life in the Ancient Maya World*, 197.
37. Foster, *Handbook to Life in the Ancient Maya World*, 165-66.
38. Tate, *Yaxchilan: the Design of a Maya Ceremonial City*, 33.
39. Ibid., 37.

# 11 ~ Bonampak

1. Peter Mathews, "Epigrafía de la Región del Usumacinta," *Arqueología Mexicana*, vol. IV, num. 22 (Nov.-Dec. 1996), 15.
2. Andrew Coe, *Archaeological Mexico* (Chico: Moon Publications, 1998), 259.
3. Ibid.
4. Ibid.
5. Lynn V. Foster, *Handbook to Life in the Ancient Maya World* (New York: Oxford University Press, 2005), 104.
6. Simon Martin and Nikolai Grube, *Chronicle of the Maya Kings and Queens* (London: Thames & Hudson, 2000), 135.
7. Mary Miller, "Bonampak, Nuevas Claves de un Enigma Ancestral," *Arqueología Mexicana*, vol. III, num. 16 (Nov.-Dec. 1995), 54.
8. Ibid.
9. Mary Miller, "Imaging Maya Art," *Secrets of the Maya* (Long Island City: Hatherleigh Press, 2003) 70.
10. Martin and Grube, *Chronicle of the Maya Kings and Queens*, 137.
11. Mathews, *Arqueología Mexicana*, 21.
12. Ibid.
13. Ibid.
14. Coe, *Archaeological Mexico*, 259.
15. Ibid., 261.
16. Miller, *Arqueología Mexicana*, 50.
17. Coe, *Archaeological Mexico*, 262.
18. Miller, *Arqueología Mexicana*, 53.
19. Miller, *Secrets of the Maya*, 68-70.

20. Martin and Grube, *Chronicle of the Maya Kings and Queens*, 136.
21. Coe, *Archaeological Mexico*, 264.
22. Ibid., 265.
23. Ibid., 266.
24. Michael D. Coe, *The Maya* (New York:Thames & Hudson Inc, 2005), 129.
25. Miller, *Secrets of the Maya*, 68.
26. See Miller, *Arqueología Mexicana*, 50-51, 55.
27. Coe, *The Maya*, 99.
28. Foster, *Handbook to Life in the Ancient Maya World*, 321-22.
29. Miller, *Secrets of the Maya*, 30.
30. Linda Schele and Peter Mathews, *The Code of Kings* (New York: Simon & Schuster, 1998), 376.
31. Robert J. Sharer with Loa P.Traxler, *The Ancient Maya* (Stanford University Press, 2006), 94.

# 12 ~ Palenque

1. Simon Martin and Nikolai Grube, *Chronicle of the Maya Kings and Queens* (London:Thames & Hudson, 2000), 156.
2. Ibid., 156-57.
3. Ibid., 42.
4. Ibid., 160-61.
5. John L. Stephens, *Incidents of Travel in Central America, Chiapas, and Yucatan*, vol. II (New York: Dover Publications, 1969), 357
6. Andrew Coe, *Archaeological Mexico* (Chico: Moon Publications, 1998), 235-36.
7. Linda Schele and Peter Mathews, *The Code of Kings*, (New York: Simon & Schuster, 1998), 104-108 and Martin and Grube, *Chronicle of the Maya Kings and Queens*, 168.
8. Coe, *Archaeological Mexico*, 239.
9. Ibid., 243.
10. Martin and Grube, *Chronicle of the Maya Kings and Queens*, 156-57.
11. See Hubert Howe Bancroft, *The Works of Hubert Howe Bancroft:The Native Races*, vol.V (San Francisco: L. Bancroft & Company, 1883), 159, 196, 219, and 621.
12. Joseph L.Allen, *Exploring the Lands of the Book of Mormon* (Orem: S.A. Publishers, 1989), 32-34.
13. See Arnoldo González Cruz and Guillermo Bernal Romero, "Grupo XVI de Palenque" and David S. Stuart, "Las Nuevas Inscripciones del Templo XIX, Palenque," *Arqueología Mexicana*, vol.VIII, num. 45 (September-October 2000), 23 and 29-32.
14. Martin and Grube, *Chronicle of the Maya Kings and Queens*, 159.
15. Ibid., 169 and Lynn V. Foster, *Handbook to Life in the Ancient Maya World* (New York: Oxford University Press, 2005), 175.
16. Martin and Grube, *Chronicle of the Maya Kings and Queens*, 169.
17. See Coe, *Archaeological Mexico*, 240-41 and Allen J. Christianson, *The Sacred Tree of the Ancient Maya* (Provo, Utah: Maxwell Institute, 1997).
18. See Foster, *Handbook to Life in the Ancient Maya World*, 174 and Martin and Grube, *Chronicle of the Maya Kings and Queens*, 169.
19. Schele and Mathews, *The Code of Kings*, 132.
20. Foster, Handbook to *Life in the Ancient Maya World*, 197.
21. Schele and Mathews, *The Code of Kings*, 167, 246.
22. Ibid., 110-19.
23. Foster, *Handbook to Life in the Ancient Maya World*, 165-66.
24. L.Taylor Hansen, *He Walked the Americas* (Amherst:Amherst Press, 1964), 173-75.
25. Schele and Mathews, *The Code of Kings*, 201; Bancroft, *The Native Races*, vol.V, 621.
26. Bancroft, *The Native Races*, vol.V, 188.
27. Foster, *Handbook to Life in the Ancient Maya World*, 163-64.
28. Ibid., 160.

29. See Allen, *Exploring the Lands of the Book of Mormon*, 118-28 and Diane E. Wirth, *A Challenge to the Critics* (Bountiful, Utah: Horizon Publishers, 1986), 65-75.
30. Schele and Mathews, *The Code of Kings*, 35.
31. Foster, *Handbook to Life in the Ancient Maya World*, 309-10.
32. Ibid., 184.
33. Ibid., 176.
34. Ibid., 177.
35. Schele and Mathews, *The Code of Kings*, 116, 210.
36. David S. Stuart, "Las Nuevas Inscripciones del Templo XIX, Palenque," *Arqueología Mexicana*, vol. VIII, num. 45 (Sept.-Oct. 2000), 30.
37. Ibid.
38. Ibid., 33.

# 13 - Tikal

1. Peter D. Harrison, *The Lords of Tikal* (London: Thames & Hudson, 1999), 9, 30.
2. Linda Schele and Peter Mathews, *The Code of Kings* (New York: Simon & Schuster, 1998), 63-64.
3. Vilma Fialko, "Tikal, Guatemala: La Cabeza del Reino de los Hijos del Sol y del Agua," *Arqueología Mexicana*, vol. XI, num. 66 (Mar.-Apr. 2004), 40.
4. Schele and Mathews, *The Code of Kings*, 64.
5. Ibid., 63.
6. Harrison, *The Lords of Tikal*, 9.
7. Ibid.
8. Ibid.
9. Tom Gidwitz, "Pioneers of the Bajo," *Secrets of the Maya* (Long Island City: Hatherleigh Press, 2003), 168.
10. Schele and Mathews, *The Code of Kings*, 63-65.
11. Harrison, *The Lords of Tikal*, 65-66.
12. Ibid.
13. Ibid.
14. Schele and Mathews, *The Code of Kings*, 66.
15. Lynn V. Foster, *Handbook to Life in the Ancient Maya World* (New York: Oxford University Press, 2005), 42.
16. Ibid., 94.
17. Harrison, *The Lords of Tikal*, 78.
18. Ibid., 126.
19. Schele and Mathews, *The Code of Kings*, 70.
20. Ibid.
21. Harrison, *The Lords of Tikal*, 68.
22. Ibid., 82.
23. Ibid., 66.
24. Ibid., 192.
25. Oswaldo Chinchilla Mazariegos, "Arqueología y Medio Ambiente del Petén," *Arqueología Mexicana*, 20-21.
26. Harrison, *The Lords of Tikal*, 200.
27. Schele and Mathews, *The Code of Kings*, 90.
28. Foster, *Handbook to Life in the Ancient Maya World*, 209.
29. Simon Martin and Nikolai Grube, *Chronicle of the Maya Kings and Queens* (London: Thames & Hudson, 2000), 50.
30. Ibid., 147.
31. Harrison, *The Lords of Tikal*, 56.

32. John Montgomery, *Tikal: An Illustrated History of the Ancient Maya Capital* (New York: Hippocrene Books, Inc., 2001) 25.
33. Harrison, *The Lords of Tikal*, 48.
34. Ibid., 55.
35. Ibid., 186.
36. Ibid., 167–70.
37. Foster, *Handbook to Life in the Ancient Maya World*, 209.
38. Harrison, *The Lords of Tikal*, 48.
39. See Linda Schele and David Friedel, *A Forest of Kings* (New York: Morrow, 1990), 198 and color plate 1.
40. Martin and Grube, *Chronicle of the Maya Kings and Queens*, 44.
41. Harrison, *The Lords of Tikal*, 142.
42. Ibid., 142–43.
43. Ibid., 142.
44. Ibid., 114, 184.
45. Ibid., 73.
46. Martin and Grube, *Chronicle of the Maya Kings and Queens*, 48.
47. Harrison, *The Lords of Tikal*, 159.
48. Ibid., 160–61.
49. Ibid., 161.
50. Martin and Grube, *Chronicle of the Maya Kings and Queens*, 42.
51. Ibid.
52. See Fialko, "Tikal, Guatemala: La Cabeza del Reino de los Hijos del Sol y del Agua," 36.
53. Montgomery, *Tikal: An Illustrated History of the Ancient Maya Capital*, 8.
54. Fialko, "Tikal, Guatemala: La Cabeza del Reino de los Hijos del Sol y del Agua," 40, 42.
55. Montgomery, *Tikal: An Illustrated History of the Ancient Maya Capital*, 25.
56. William R. Coe, *Tikal: A Handbook of the Ancient Maya Ruins* (Guatemala: Centro Impresor Piedra Santa, 1988), 43.
57. Ibid., 28.
58. Schele and Mathews, *The Code of Kings*, 70.
59. Schele and Friedel, *A Forest of Kings*, 164.
60. Foster, *Handbook to Life in the Ancient Maya World*, 155.
61. Schele and Friedel, *A Forest of Kings*, 147.
62. Ibid., 159.
63. Foster, *Handbook to Life in the Ancient Maya World*, 41–42.
64. Harrison, *The Lords of Tikal*, 68.
65. Ibid., 122.
66. Robert J. Sharer with Loa P. Traxler, *The Ancient Maya* (Stanford University Press, 2006), 387.
67. Harrison, *The Lords of Tikal*, 195.
68. Martin and Grube, *Chronicle of the Maya Kings and Queens*, 49.
69. See John L. Stephens, *Incidents of Travel in Yucatan*, vol. 1 (New York: Dover Publications, Inc., 1963), 102–03, 252.
70. Fialko, "Tikal, Guatemala: La Cabeza del Reino de los Hijos del Sol y del Agua," 41.
71. Harrison, *The Lords of Tikal*, 91.
72. Ibid., 190.
73. Ibid., 191.
74. Montgomery, *Tikal: An Illustrated History of the Ancient Maya Capital*, 12..

# 14 - Yaxhá

1. Michael D. Coe, *The Maya* (New York: Thames & Hudson Inc, 2005), 9.
2. Bernard Hermes, "Arte en Material Malacológico en la Laguna Yaxhá, Guatemala," *Arqueología*

*Mexicana*, vol. XI, num. 66 (Mar.–Apr. 2004), 74.

3. Robert J. Sharer with Loa P. Traxler, *The Ancient Maya* (Stanford University Press, 2006), 688.

4. See Tom Gidwitz, "Pioneers of the Bajo," *Secrets of the Maya* (Long Island City: Hatherleigh Press, 2003), 166-69.

5. John S. Henderson, *The World of the Ancient Maya* (Ithaca and London: Cornell University Press, 1997), 160.

6. Coe, *The Maya*, 102.

7. Bernard Hermes and Gustavo Martínez, "El Clásico Terminal en el Área de la Laguna Yaxha, Petén," *XVIII Simposio de Investigaciones Arqueológicas en Guatemala*, 2004, 5.

8. Simon Martin and Nikolai Grube, *Chronicle of the Maya Kings and Queens* (London: Thames & Hudson, 2000), 82.

9. Hermes and Martínez, "El Clásico Terminal en el Área de la Laguna Yaxha, Petén," 5.

10. Ibid., 5-6.

11. Ibid., 7.

12. Sharer with Traxler, *The Ancient Maya*, 617.

13. Hermes, "Arte en Material Malacológico en la Laguna Yaxhá, Guatemala," 75.

14. Sharer with Traxler, *The Ancient Maya*, 375.

15. Hermes, "Arte en Material Malacológico en la Laguna Yaxhá, Guatemala," 77.

16. Hermes and Martínez, "El Clásico Terminal en el Área de la Laguna Yaxha, Petén," 4.

17. Hermes, "Arte en Material Malacológico en la Laguna Yaxhá, Guatemala," 75.

18. David Stuart, "The Yaxha Emblem Glyph as Yax-ha," *Research Reports on Ancient Maya Writing 1* (Washington, D.C.: Center for Maya Research, 1985), 4-5.

19. Ibid., 1, 4.

20. Ibid., 5.

21. Martin and Grube, *Chronicle of the Maya Kings and Queens*, 82.

22. Gidwitz, "Pioneers of the Bajo," 168.

# 15 – Quiriguá

1. Simon Martin and Nikolai Grube, Chronicle of the Maya Kings and Queens (London: Thames & Hudson, 2000), 219.

2. Robert J. Sharer with Loa P. Traxler, *The Ancient Maya* (Stanford University Press, 2006), 352.

3. Ibid., 333.

4. Ibid., 252.

5. See Christopher Jones and Robert J. Sharer, "Archaeological Investigations in the Site Core of Quirigua," 11-12; Wendy Ashmore, "Discovering Early Classic Quirigua," 35, Expedition, vol. 23 no. 1 (Fall 1980).

6. Martin and Grube, *Chronicle of the Maya Kings and Queens*, 216-17.

7. Ibid., 218.

8. Ibid. 217-18.

9. Sharer with Traxler, *The Ancient Maya*, 415, 482.

10. Martin and Grube, *Chronicle of the Maya Kings and Queens*, 218-19.

11. John S. Henderson, The World of the Ancient Maya (Ithaca and London: Cornell University Press, 1997), 176-77.

12. Martin and Grube, *Chronicle of the Maya Kings and Queens*, 219.

13. Ibid., 222.

14. Sharer with Traxler, *The Ancient Maya*, 495.

15. Martin and Grube, *Chronicle of the Maya Kings and Queens*, 224-25.

16. Sharer with Traxler, *The Ancient Maya*, 579.

17. Ibid., 352.

18. See Ashmore, "Discovering Early Classic Quirigua," 35-37.

19. Martin and Grube, *Chronicle of the Maya Kings and Queens*, 221.
20. See Jones and Sharer, "Archaeological Investigations in the Site Core of Quirigua," 18-19.
21. Sharer with Traxler, *The Ancient Maya*, 353-54.
22. Martin and Grube, *Chronicle of the Maya Kings and Queens*, 217.
23. Ibid.
24. See Ashmore, "The Classic Maya Settlement at Quirigua," Expedition vol. 23 no. 1 (Fall 1980), 20.
25. John L. Stephens, *Incidents of Travel in Central America, Chiapas, and Yucatan*, vol. I (New York: Dover Publications, 1969), 153 and vol. II, 441-42.
26. See Linda Schele and David Freidel, *A Forest of Kings* (New York: HarperCollins Publishers, 1990), 90-91.
27. Ibid., 19, 164.
28. Ibid., 145, 260.
29. See Linda Schele and Peter Mathews, *The Code of Kings* (New York: Simon & Schuster, 1998), 236, 249, 358; Lynn V. Foster, *Handbook to Life in the Ancient Maya World* (New York: Oxford University Press, 2005), 168.
30. *Times and Seasons*, Vol. III, No. 23, 1 October 1842, 927.
31. Ashmore, "The Classic Maya Settlement at Quirigua," 24.

# 17 - Copán

1. Linda Schele and Peter Mathews, *The Code of Kings* (New York: Simon & Schuster, 1998), 134.
2. Ibid., 139.
3. José Pérez de Lara, "Guía de Viajeros: Copán, Honduras," *Arqueología Mexicana*, vol. XI, num. 66 (Mar.–Apr. 2004), 82.
4. William L. Fash and Barbara Fash, "La Ciudad de Copán, Honduras: Arte y Escritura Mayas," *Arqueología Mexicana*, vol. XI, num. 66 (Mar.–Apr. 2004), 65.
5. Ibid.
6. See John M. Longyear III, "The Ethnological Significance of Copan Pottery," *The Maya and Their Neighbors* (New York: Dover Publications, Inc., 1977), 268-71.
7. Schele and Mathews, *The Code of Kings*, 133.
8. Ibid., 134.
9. John S. Henderson, *The World of the Ancient Maya* (Ithaca and London: Cornell University Press, 1997), 163.
10. Ibid., 176.
11. Schele and Mathews, *The Code of Kings*, 134.
12. Henderson, *The World of the Ancient Maya*, 164.
13. Ibid., 170.
14. Schele and Mathews, *The Code of Kings*, 170.
15. Ibid., 349.
16. Henderson, *The World of the Ancient Maya*, 170.
17. Schele and Mathews, *The Code of Kings*, 170-71.
18. Henderson, *The World of the Ancient Maya*, 171.
19. Ibid., 39.
20. Ibid., 142, 39.
21. Jeremy A. Sabloff, *The New Archaeology and the Ancient Maya* (New York: W. H. Freeman and Company, 1990), 109.
22. Henderson, *The World of the Ancient Maya*, 233, 235.
23. de Lara, *Arqueología Mexicana*, 82-83.
24. John L. Stephens, *Incidents of Travel in Central America, Chiapas, and Yucatan*, vol. I (New York: Dover Publications, 1969), 99, 132.
25. Ibid., 160.

## Endnotes

26. de Lara, *Arqueología Mexicana*, 83.
27. Ibid., and Sabloff, *The New Archaeology and the Ancient Maya*, 160.
28. de Lara, *Arqueología Mexicana*, 83 and Sabloff, *The New Archaeology and the Ancient Maya*, 161-63.
29. Sabloff, *The New Archaeology and the Ancient Maya*, 160.
30. See Stephens, *Incidents of Travel in Central America, Chiapas, and Yucatan*, vol. I, 133.
31. Schele and Mathews, *The Code of Kings*, 135.
32. Ibid., 346.
33. de Lara, *Arqueología Mexicana*, 85.
34. Henderson, *The World of the Ancient Maya*, 164.
35. Ibid., 165-66.
36. Schele and Mathews, *The Code of Kings*, 158.
37. Ibid., 160-61.
38. Ibid., 163.
39. Ibid., 143-45.
40. See Lynn V. Foster, *Handbook to Life in the Ancient Maya World* (New York: Oxford University Press, 2005), 205, 208.
41. Schele and Mathews, *The Code of Kings*, 171-72.
42. Henderson, *The World of the Ancient Maya*, 165.
43. Schele and Mathews, *The Code of Kings*, 348.
44. Ibid., 154.
45. Ibid., 158.
46. Ibid., 136-38.
47. Robert J. Sharer with Loa P. Traxler, *The Ancient Maya* (Stanford University Press, 2006), 487.
48. Fash and Fash, *Arqueología Mexicana*, 68.
49. Michael D. Coe, *The Maya* (New York: Thames & Hudson Inc, 2005), 105.
50. de Lara, *Arqueología Mexicana*, 87.
51. Sharer with Traxler, *The Ancient Maya*, 491.
52. See Schele and Mathews, *The Code of Kings*, 145.
53. Ibid., 143, 145, 158, 162.
54. Ibid., 167.
55. Ibid., 145.
56. Ibid., 143.
57. Ibid., 155.
58. Sharer with Traxler, *The Ancient Maya*, 726.
59. Ibid., 148.
60. Foster, *Handbook to Life in the Ancient Maya World*, 286.
61. See Sharer with Traxler, *The Ancient Maya*, 116-17.
62. See Schele and Mathews, *The Code of Kings*, 160.